To

prof Gordon Farmer

from

Ifeanyi onwuka.

An Introduction To Positive Life Lessons

Ifeanyi Onwuka

AuthorHouse™
1663 Liberty Drive, Suite 200
Bloomington, IN 47403
www.authorhouse.com
Phone: 1-800-839-8640

First published by AuthorHouse 7/14/2008

ISBN: 978-1-4343-6624-5 (sc)

Printed in the United States of America
Bloomington, Indiana

This book is printed on acid-free paper.

Dedication

This book is dedicated with love to my wonderful wife, Ifeoma, who has always been my strength and my source of inspiration and happiness and to my cute little daughter, Seonna, who would always lie in her cot and watch me closely while I do my work. Thank you for that superb motivation.

Acknowledgements

To my editor: Michael, for his sharp eyes and good wits.

To Yvette: for all her effort towards publishing the book.

To my father and stepmother: Prof (Rev) & Mrs N.D.K. Onwuka, for their constant prayers for me which have always been guiding me. Thank you for your encouragement.

To my father-in-law: Prof P.N. Okeke, for his experienced advice and great sense of humour and to my mother-in-law: Prof (Mrs) F.N. Okeke, for her relentless effort towards typing of this work and to see that the book becomes reality.

To my brothers; Nwachukwu, Nnaemeka, Neme and Kosi and my sisters: Adaobi, Akachukwu, Uchechukwu, Chidera and Onyi for always being there for me.

To Amobi Okoye: for his special advice based on the entire work.

To my friends: Justin, Tim, Iloba, Ekene and the rest who have always been there for me.

To Emma Mills, for your good advice and showing enthusiasm in the work.

To my various aunties: Com, Baby, Nwando, Nkechi, Obiamaka and Adaeze for their support.

To all my numerous cousins who have always being there for me.

Contents

Preamble

This book is a guide towards self-realization and it starts off by telling you how a man is born and the struggles that ultimately challenge him as he decides where he wants to be.

I have used certain topics to emphasize beliefs and strategies that could guide you in life. Remember, it's only a guide; and therefore the contents shouldn't be followed without proper scrutiny.

My advice is that you challenge yourself as you go through the book. Some of the experiences might be similar to your circumstances and situations. Don't ignore them, look at them critically and see how you can effect a positive change in your life.

Try as much as possible to go through the book more than once, because the more you read, the more clues you can use for problem solving.

Map out a stepwise approach towards your goals and go for it. Don't fall into the shadows of procrastination, because this won't lead you anywhere.

I have always thought about helping others, especially people who have succumbed to the pressures of modern society and have given up. This is a way of saying that there is hope out there. The point is; life can be an enjoyable journey if you start now to look at your life in general.

Be wise about life and embrace your conscience as your guide. Most of us neglect our 'little angels' and seek answers elsewhere while we have the solutions within.

You are the light that could shine on others and effect a change in them for the better. If you hadn't thought about this before, then start now.

If you can imagine being in a world all alone, terrorized by your fears, haunted by your ambitions, always reminded of your misfortunes, basically not knowing who you are, I believe this book is for you. Good luck.

This book will definitely touch many lives that positively seek self-fulfilment through discipline and hard work. The choice is yours.

CHAPTER ONE

A man is born

A man is born into the deep heart of reality with so many struggles during the gestational period. Finally, a child emerges into this world full of uncertain events. The cries of this helpless child and the distressed mother all trigger a joyous moment at the time of birth. But, at the time of birth, how does one analyse such thoughts as we await the coming of the young one? It is the interplay of anxiety, emotions and reflection of who we are. Such thoughts are those of a kind that we are obliged to play on, to fulfil our wishful thinking. We long for the young one for nine months and, having awaited the arrival of the young one, at that very moment, our wish fulfilment is somewhat of an amazing journey. Our stream of thoughts is that of an endless search for how we were created. It's amazing how nature has given rise to such an extraordinary creature with endless possibilities of an approach to life. If you recall being on the hospital premises and awaiting the arrival of a young child, you will totally understand the extent of the drama that takes place in one's mind.

The search for who we are starts at that very moment when a foetus is formed. It is an amazing journey throughout the gestational period. But that is just the start of our journey towards the origin of our existence. I am not going to explore the matter of evolution but rather, I would suggest that as of the present moment, the children of today are somewhat different from those of the past and this is due to evolutionary trends.

This child begins his first journey in life as he learns how to feed. He then sets out to learn certain behavioural qualities that lead him through life. Such a behavioural tendency is tied in with his innate behaviour. Others are acquired through learning from society. I remember being briefed on how to behave when I was a child: the endless cries that triggered certain emotional turmoil in my mum. With so much care and dedication, she decided to let go and put me to the test. Her ideas were those of classical conditioning, as Pavlov stated in his theory, which entailed leaving me in front of the television with cartoons flashing here and there. To her utmost surprise, those cries subsided to the point where not only did I concentrate on the programme but also slept gracefully. To my mum, it was an emotional experience, because it did entail leaving me on my own to cry till I dropped off. But that was a harsh reality to embrace. Even though the psychological implications were many, it did help my mum establish a routine for me as well as giving her time to perform her domestic duties. In effect, I learnt the hard way through acquired learning, but my innate behaviour did express itself through the wondrous cries and screams. Seeing this from a different angle, my learning phase started at that point, but for others it could have started later or earlier.

As the child grows, he learns certain behaviours, which lead him through life. Behavioural learning depends on several factors, such as the psyche of the individual, the people around him (culture) and society. This means the people around him and society will have a tremendous effect on his behavioural capabilities. Culture is seen as the way or life of the people. The life of the people is literally what the individual perceives and believe in. Certain precepts he believes, others he rejects. Culture dates back through generations. Different cultures have different ways of seeing things. Believing in a culture is another phase towards self-development. If the child sees and believes in a certain culture, it then becomes part and parcel of him. Some of it he believes and other parts of it he rejects in the fight to really understand who he is. The growth of the child is the work of biochemistry, as we have been informed, and for this to effectively take place; we need to physically ingest 'edibles'. These have been put there to nourish the body cells, which is in harmony with the entire system of mankind. To reject the power of such a habit would be to starve nature and in effect drive mankind to death. These cells are the building blocks of our mental structure, enabling us to assimilate knowledge and know more about existence. We need to know more about how to open all the doors to human reasoning and understanding. If we know how the human mind works then we will have the key to unlock our intelligence. Such concepts are the truth behind our lives and, for us to enjoy nature's gift of intelligence, we need to know more about these concepts. Some scientists have put them forward as the intelligence quotient, which grades us on how intelligent we might be. It is on a scale such that when ascertained it can be used as a reference point. Nature has designed the whole body system to fit into this periphery of life; therefore an understanding of how human nature works is vital in unravelling the mysteries behind our existence. Personality development comes with time, but man's surroundings have a major influence on his psyche. Such influence may have positive or negative effects on self-attainment. A society that believes in hard work will definitely have a positive effect on the psyche of the individual, while a society that rejects hard work will have a negative effect on the individual's psyche. This invariably will have an effect on the personality development of the society at large. As this child reaches the age of reasoning, he then decides his views about life. This would tie in with his peers, the society, his family and his 'self'. 'Self' here encompasses all components that actually make him who he is, from body cells to a whole being. That quality which he acquired through his 'active learning phase' affects his personality. That personality, marked by the influence of society and consolidated by his peers, sets him out on the right or wrong path. Personality formation is the sum total of a person's character. Many theories evolve; some break through. Such success in personality formation is tied in with the components of the person's character. As one progresses into this phase, man's personality shows influences from olden times to modern times. Changes in the society have left deep marks on the new society with its different cultural mixes and religions.

At times, it has become a place of war and peace, with different opinions jittering in a clash of speech conquests. Realists could voice their opinions as the clash of different views whereas modern society deems it a racial 'slur'. The amount of sludge in society is vast, with all kinds of different views aired and reaching eager ears. In a society like this, the child adopts certain characteristics, aligns it with what he chooses, embraces it and then moves on. As it stands, these norms could be right or wrong, but to the child it is the order of the day. Certain core values in a certain society could be ascertained as wrong in the eyes of the accuser, but in the real sense of it, it could be right. How do we justify what is right or wrong and then transfer these thoughts of reasoning to our youth? The obvious answer would be to adhere to society's values. Societal values in modern times have shifted from the real to the hypothetical. With so much hope invested in matters of vanity in the search for things we don't have. Those things we don't have are basically things we don't need. We have overlooked the basic needs of man and have clouded our minds with materialism, which in effect haunts every facet of our financial planning. I call it a silent thief in a million pockets that challenges our way of life. People have choices and so on, and they abide by these choices. The societal choices are shifting towards non-values and consequently causing major behavioural changes. The way an individual behaves is attributed mainly to his surroundings. In Africa, people embrace religion as a way of life. This is the norm of the society, but with so much westernised influence, such extremes of hate and love have given rise to a controversial debate threatening cultural derailment with changes both to the society and the individual. Man has evolved with so many characteristics; therefore such traits could be the start of a personality catastrophe or a blessing. Believing in such precepts can be dicey, although it's left for the individual to decide. A man is born into the heart of struggle with such confusion of dos and don'ts, yet he finally settles for the better. What are your views about different cultural mixes and the effect this has on personality formation? These are a few examples of questions that could stimulate your mind.

- How is it that with different cultures coexisting in the same community the world hasn't collapsed yet?
- With different cultures emanating from different continents, are there advantages and disadvantages associated with these diffferent cultures?
- Why are there different cultures?
- How does your culture influence you in terms of personality formation?
- Are we 'culture aware'?

I believe with different cultures cohabiting in one domain, there are bound to be differences. I suggest you take your time and learn about them because some of these influences can be a positive lesson in your life. Don't reject them because you think your own culture is better. In life, it is all about living together as one and reaching greater heights. Did you know that without the different cultural mixes and unification strategies, we wouldn't have known about Egypt and its history? Think about that.

Positive Lessons 1

- The birth of a man signifies his essence on the planet.
- Our behaviour stems from our inner self; others acquired through learning.
- Culture is seen as the way or life of the people and this actually reflects people's behaviour.
- If a child adopts all the precepts of a particular culture, it will surely become his way of living.
- A personality marked by society's influence and consolidated by one's peers, sets a person out on the right or wrong path.
- Changes in societal structures have left deep marks in the new society with its different cultures and religions.
- Materialism is a silent thief in a million pockets that challenges our way of life.
- Our society is constantly embracing non-values as ideals, without acknowledging the warning signs of nature.
- Personality development comes with time, but remember, it could change for the better.
- A society that believes in hard work will definitely influence the psyche of the common man.
- If a child misses out on the active learning phase of life, problems of under-achievement will become the face of an unmarked endeavour.
- The problem with our society is the way we bring up our youth. Those parents who are at fault experience the repercussions at an unexpected time.
- The problem with us is our lack of understanding of human nature.

CHAPTER TWO

The Power of Positive Thought

The power of positive thought not only aligns you with what is right and is right for you, but also prepares you for the unexpected which is unavoidable. Man chooses his ways in life, and the choices he makes could be positive or negative which in effect reflect in his attitude. Some thoughts he consciously accepts while others he rejects. The power to choose or reject reflects who you are. For you to cross the bridge of success through devoted hard work, you need to relax and accept changes in life. Choices are made and, for these choices to manifest themselves practically, you need to adhere to them strongly. If you sincerely listen to yourself, through reflective moments, you will definitely become one of the modern champions of today. Your fate is in your hands. Leave it alone and it will definitely return to haunt you. Don't become one of those millions of souls out there who wished the clock could be turned back because, in a split of a second, they realised they might have achieved so much. For several reasons, including the so-called 'free spirit' I do what I like attitude, it is quite obvious why such misfortunes manifest in our modern day and age. 'Seeing is believing as doing is mastering'. As such, understanding yourself and preparing to change your attitudes towards positive thinking will lead you to near-perfection and excellence in your wishes.

From an observational point of view, people think differently and that is why we are humans. But the problem arises when we think negatively. Such thoughts arise due to circumstances we can change, while others we cannot change and these are reflected in our daily lives. Effecting a positive change in people's lives is quite hard. This is because the problem might be deep-rooted in the hearts of the individuals in question. Mostly, people who are affected take it as a way of living and then embrace such misconceptions. They dwell on this world with self-pity and a negative outlook. Life to them is just another terrible journey. The good news for you is that your life can be changed if you believe in the power of positive thoughts. Man, as he is, has the gift of understanding, which comes from birth. To use this gift would be to maximize your highest potential of becoming 'you'. With this, you can become one of the most influential people on the planet, just by understanding 'who' you are. I remember a day in 1983, as the most influential day of my life. That was the day my mother kicked the bucket and passed on to glory. It was a sad moment not just for me but also for all who knew her. As a child, at that very moment, I felt cheated, withdrawn, sad and dejected. I could not possibly think straight, since it all happened very suddenly. One minute everything was fine; the next moment it was all about hospitals and death certificates. To me it was devastating because my hope of becoming someone had just gone in a flash. Imagine yourself in such a situation, with circumstances around you changing for the worse. I couldn't even coordinate myself, because to me it was all over. There was no fight left in me, due to such a catastrophic situation. To me everything then seemed to be a mirage. The more I approached situations, the more I realized there was no fight in me. It got to a point where, I would say, I was 'really low', but because I listened to myself and had a lot of reflective thoughts, it became clear to me why my mum had died. If I had decided to wallow in self-pity, then I would definitely have become a practical failure in the modern day, but if I stood and adopted a positive attitude, then it would become a tale of moral lessons. Why did all this happen? It was a little voice, which said that my mother wanted me to be educated and, if I failed her, it would be a disgrace on my part. This was the motivation I was waiting for. As a result of this revelation, I have excelled in my career as a pharmacist to date. Why am I narrating these stories? This will be just like a speck in some people's eyes, but to me it was everything. Therefore, if you think you have been waiting for that special moment that could change your life for the better, then this is your chance.

- Take a close look at yourself. At a glance, what do you see?
- Ask several questions about your life; for example, it could be about your marriage, your job etc.
- Ask yourself, where am I now, and where do I want to be in 10 years time?
- Are you on the right track towards becoming a better person?
- Is there is any black cloud over your head you need to address?

All these are questions you need to ask yourself. But when you are ready to enter the next phase towards self-actualization, you will definitely know.

The power of positive thinking can manifest itself in many ways, starting from a single step towards changing your old ways. I have had a lot of experiences in my life, which is a lesson for many who have fallen; but haven't risen. I once thought of becoming an American pharmacist, and had my thoughts towards making a lot of money with the whole boom of the pharmaceutical industry in America. Firstly, I had a lot of documents and forms, which I had to go through, and consequently sent many documents to the pharmacy board in America. I made my first payment in cash, and to me this was something new. I was happy that the job was surely there for me. After a few months, I received letters stating the date of the examination and that it was scheduled for New York City, during the winter season. This

I did not mind because I was really getting into the whole scenario. The date came, I went, took the examination and passed, but there was something more. I was told that I had to take this oral English examination to complete the assessment. I decided to do just that, but to my utmost amazement I failed. It now became a matter of how many times I had to sit down and go through these boring examinations. My ultimate examination was on the same subject, but with so much anticipation and nervousness, I decided to have my last go, but it never happened. It was as if I was chasing a shadow that was never there. The day before the examination came, I realized that there was something wrong. I called the customer service department and was told that I had not applied for the examination. She further went on to say that even though my name did appear on the list, for some reason, which was not clear to her, there seemed to be a problem. This was the most shocking experience I have ever had for a long time. There I sat, with my hands across my head, as millions of thoughts flashed across my mind in a second. To them, it was another disappointment, but to me it was a reality. Was I going to America to become a 'rich' pharmacist or was I going there to influence health care matters in general? At that moment, I knew that the purpose of the whole journey towards becoming an American pharmacist was a fluke. If I had listened to myself I probably wouldn't have embarked on this fruitless journey. And because I was going for the wrong reasons, which had no positive effect in life in general, it was a failure even before it began. The search for something new emerged, as I found out; I was to become a writer and something more in life. It was then that I realized how destiny still stands even in the midst of all eventualities. Thought processes are there for us to use to effect a positive change in our lives. Fear of the unknown still stands as one of the most devastating drives towards self-realization of one's dream, don't you think?

If you embrace your fears and make them your strengths, then success should definitely be within your reach. Work on them each day slowly and you will be amazed at your success. Ensure you set realistic goals that are achievable, not just for the sake of setting yourself targets and abandoning them. If your daily task is to feed on positivity, then it will become part of your existence. Time is precious, as they say, but time is still on your side if you start now. Procrastination should be viewed as a thing of the past, but hard work and dedication should be of the present. Don't let people with clouds of negativity embrace every facet of your life. This is because, as you are settling out to forsake the past for the present, you must always remember that the past might express itself in different ways. Avoid negative people as much as you can, listen to positive people, seek advice, build your own self-esteem and shine like a dazzling star. Remember not to let failure be the answer to unwanted excuses. Capitalize on your weakness and you will be amazed at how strong they might turn out to be.

The power of the mind is unlimited. Seek constantly to challenge your mind, because whatever your mind believes in can be achievable. Deceptive thoughts are there to constantly remind us of our failures. Defeat them; don't let them ruin your life. The downfall of a man, they say, is not the end of his life; rather, it is a positive step towards the start of something great. Great minds think alike is a saying, but remember that great thoughts came from minds like yours. Effect a positive change and make your life worth living. Your life has just begun if something new emerges from positive thinking. Wallowing in the so-called dreams towards detriment will not only stigmatize your essence but will also tarnish your reputation. If you set out on a journey towards the realization of your dreams towards positive thoughts, you will escape the 'band wagons' of self-pity. You are, so to speak, the epitaph of your existence. Keep it going.

I have decided to devise three strategies, which will effectively change your life. I have called them the three steps towards positive thinking.

STEP 1: Stop and think strategy

Due to the modern pressures of daily living, man has transgressed from doing what he likes, to the computer age, with so many machines at work; he has become attached to his 'toys'. A friend of mine once asked me, 'Are we actually living in a world of machines or humans?' And, from that, I saw where he was coming from: a world full of machines, which man has to deal with. That is just the beginning of problems for man. With so many pressures from the modern world, he has learnt to adapt to changes very quickly; this is because of his intuitive behaviour and adaptive capabilities, which have made him a survivor. In effect, he has now become a modern man who works in an office in a city and has forgotten that, once, we all had to rear cattle and worked as farmers. The point here is, man has reasons for his existence and, if he pushes himself beyond the limits of reality, he may become a 'zombie' of modern times.

The year 2002 for me was a year of self-examination. As I unravelled the mysteries of the story I heard, I began to ponder upon my life. It was all about working and earning a living. But when you begin to push yourself beyond certain boundaries, then get ready to accept debilitating consequences as regards to your health. A friend of mine sneaked in a story about his neighbour who had, shockingly, collapsed on a train; he explained how he had been involved with two jobs and was never at home. He was always tired and snatched his sleep as he took his breaks. He once told my friend that he slept in-between jobs and breaks and that he was practically a 'walking shadow'. The moral of the story is to pay attention to your needs and attend to them in terms of priority and not desirability. But, at the same time, be careful how you search for materialistic needs because it could limit your sense of reasoning. As many of us are culprits of this sad existence, be warned and learn. I thought about the whole scenario and it made me realize one thing. I had to first establish where I wanted to be and then plan around it. I thought about what my friend's neighbour might be saying to himself in the next world: 'Have I done my daily duties to the point of no return?' His unconscious mind may not be questioned, but his motives and how he must have gone about it might be. The problem he had was that he dwelled in the realms of modern pressures and became one of its victims. Not only had he fallen victim to it, but also 'his victim' had had a better part of him to the point of death. Had he thought about what effect he was having on his health in general, he would have definitely thought twice about it. You can work hard and achieve great things, but others can work smart and reach even greater heights. Are you in the category of those working too hard with much input but little output? Or are you in the category with little input and maximum output? I am not suggesting that one should not work hard, but be smart about it.

You have possibilities which are endless in life, but revealing the mysteries behind such possibilities can be achieved if one follows simple little steps. Because people do not think about what they are doing in life, they seem to follow others without first thinking about themselves. Imagine working for someone all your life, and suddenly finding out you have the qualities of a leader who can influence other people. At that point, you will be very disappointed because, if you had tapped those qualities you have, it would have made you one of the champions of today. A lot of people are on this treadmill and the moment they start realizing themselves, the better it is for the society at large. If you count the millions of people with forgone talents who never harnessed those talents, it would be like counting the whole world on a pair of hands. The facts are clear, the reasoning is simple: every one of us on this planet has got special talents and it is left to you and me to find out what these talents are. Mr **A** might be good at dancing; this does not necessarily mean that Mr **B** is also good at it. Mr **B** might have other gifts that will impress Mr **A.** We remark that we are all special people with different talents and aspirations.

Remember to follow your heart and intuition as you progress. We do act instinctively at times and that is one of the qualities of human nature. Man decides where he wants to act, acts according to certain ideals, performs certain tasks and then waits for his rewards. There is nothing like performing with maximum capabilities. I have witnessed from my experiences that frequent psychological challenges that aid towards improving our mental capabilities ultimately open doors that had not been used before. In effect, when you explore such realms of our existence, you will begin to perceive another mindset towards self-fulfilment. Teach yourself the lessons of life and you will find out that the more you achieve, the better it becomes. But remember, there are times when you want to embrace perfection. Yes, it is good to attain to such levels, but when it comes in the way of not achieving your goals, that's when perfect isn't good enough. Don't fall for the pressures of today and loose your special gifts forever.

These are the things you can do to uncover who you are:

(i) Have reflective moments; this will be discussed in later chapters.
(ii) Discuss with your friends, family and teachers at school your strengths and weaknesses.
(iii) Always accept your failures and work on them.
(iv) Don't let the pressures of life distract your peace.
(v) Set out to be calm and be at peace with yourself.
(vi) Always remember the laws of Karma.
(vii) Your health is in your hands. Guard it.
(viii) Be truthful to yourself.
(ix) Set realistic targets.

At all times, encourage yourself, because you will definitely meet obstacles along the way.

On the other hand, certain people can't think at all. They find it very challenging to think, because they have never thought in certain directions.

They opt for the easy way out all the time. Believe it or not, but there are a lot of people whose existence needs questioning. The solution for them is to first realize they have a problem and then to act upon any decision-making process that could lead to a change. How can you delegate a classroom task to an individual who has never been in a classroom, let alone get him to write an essay on things that matter to him? It would be a clash between the realms of conscious and unconscious, as he puzzles his way through the nasty ordeal. To him, it is mystery that can't be explained, while to the educated it is a mere assignment.

Step 1 brings you back to reality so that you can embrace things that matter .It goes further: to align you with your environment so that you can see things clearly. It seeks answers from you and helps in dealing with certain issues you normally overlook. Don't be afraid of anything; you are a special person so keep your vision alive, as you have now embraced your gifts and are ready to embark on the most amazing journey.

Decision-making ability is an essential skill which lives with us in our everyday lives. For us, to make either a right or wrong decision, we need to first think about it. Most decision-making depends on our ability to use everything available to us to make an informed judgement from our thoughts. There is this formula I use before I make a decision. I call it 'the ego tree'. What it does is that its principles ensure that our ego does not breach our sense of reasoning and therefore allows us to explore the various options left to us. The ego tree stands for neglecting man's egocentrism and concentrating on risks, outcomes, options and eventualities. When making an effective decision, this basically ensures that you are not biased when arriving at a conclusion. What goes on in our minds before a decision-making process occurs is amazing. I remember an instance when I had to change my old car. It was a matter of priority, because I didn't want to have a breakdown, as I usually engage in long-distance journeys to work. My first thought was, am I making the right decision? Secondly, if I was, did I actually know the car I wanted? I then went on to analyse the risks involved in buying a used car and how it could be either a wrong or right decision. In the end, I consulted my wife for her advice. She then gave me an option: you do have a choice; leave it and we can go back to our old wagon but your mileage is running out so it is better to make a choice on what is available. This immediately 'struck a chord', as I realized I had to change my vehicle, which I did, but it was a decision which took six hours to reach.

At times, when it comes to a decision-making process, our options overwhelm us and instil these bouts of doubts in us, so be careful not to get sucked into it. Keep at it and you will surely come out with the right decision. As I mentioned earlier, the ego tree necessitates that we effectively come to a decision. Risks are always in our way when it comes to choosing among options. Remember, risks challenge our ability to reason and to determine among many, those options that work in order to seize an opportunity. These circumstances challenge the mind and ensure that we explore all available options before making a decision. Remember, there are two sides to a risk: if you embrace it, then the closer you are revealing your wits: on the other hand, if you shy away from it, rest assured you will never reveal your inner self when it comes to challenges. Put yourself in the position of others and analyse situations, top positions and careers, and you will find out that the risks involved are many. But such positions will come to those who actively seek them. Therefore, if you come up against risks in a situation, don't shy away from it, but try as much as possible to work out if the situation is worth it; use the ego tree and work out the various options available to you. Be wise about life and keep bringing out the best in yourself.

Outcomes are there for us to cherish and work for; it is the very start of a decision-making process. Before any decision-making process can take place, there should be an outcome, which is there to challenge us, put us to the test and then wait for us to achieve our goal. I would repeat this: every effort to achieve a purpose is worth more than all the gold in a gold mine. The reason behind this stems from the reward at the very end. It is quite a fulfilling reward, because you will definitely feel the essence of living. It is good for people who solely believe in the principles of reasoning to enjoy these endless rewards. An outcome justifies the means once it is successful. To self-actualize without effective decision making would be like throwing fertile seeds into a howling wind in some barren land; in effect, it would be a waste of lives and effort. We do have a lot of options when it comes to decision-making, but when we really want to realize our dreams; it is then that we really start to understand who we really are. Chapter 9, on the crossroads analogy, explains in detail what is required of us, and how we can effectively become decision makers.

We have come to the point were we have to decide, and for us to make this decision we need the tools of life. These tools will help you. In whatever situation you find yourself, listen, understand, work and make choices among many and, in all situations; be proud of who you are so that in effect, you will begin to enjoy the aura of success. What I find very intriguing is, if you ask any child what he would like to be in future, he will definitely have an answer. But at that age, it is just admiration for some achievers; it is a mere childhood dream. But the point is; have you asked yourself the same question? Or are you still in the 'not living' phase of life? I believe that opportunities do occur, and as they occur, things begin to unfold. Brace yourself for the better or worse and always ensure you make preparation for every situation, so that unforeseen circumstances do not overwhelm you. I believe in 'self' and all its 'condiments'. Align with it and free yourself from the things that have hounded men to their graves. For effective decision-making, the ego tree will definitely find answers to your never-ending quest for self-discovery. As the words of the wise state, seek and you shall find, because if you do not seek then finding becomes difficult.

Be prepared to face a lot of obstacles along the way but, with peace at heart and determination to succeed, you will surely get there.

STEP 2: You are the enforcer of your life

My management skills were initially poor, and I always procrastinated on important matters. The time came, after so many years of financial crisis, when I then yielded to sorting my problems out. Whatever you do that involves money transfer and cash handling, it definitely entails management skills. Most of what we do these days certainly involves a lot of finances, but the question is, how many of us are very confident when managing affairs like this? The problem most of us have is that when we do have a problem situation, some of us shy away from it, instead of finding ways of solving it. Step 2 towards positive thought entails that we as individuals have to sort out our daily needs and to do this we need to start seeking answers to our daily problems and then apply them. For example, I am always late to school is a regular problem with school kids, but have I taken necessary steps to find out why? I have not taken the trouble to enforce a change, even in the light of all problems. When you try and try, and you fail, try again, because maybe you are not trying hard enough. For new ways to effect a positive change, you may need to keep trying.

Referring to the individual that is always late for school, it could be due to the following reasons:

- Always goes to bed late at night.
- Does not prepare his things before school.
- Never does his assignment on time.
- Wakes up late in the morning.
- Is not conscious of late attendance.
- Is not a studious character.

These are a few examples of what it might take to effect a positive change. Try to enforce certain behaviour tendencies that are positive and that would instil a positive personality formation. How do you enforce certain personality traits that are lacking? If you consciously believe in certain principles that could instil a good character; then start now to emulate them.

STEP 3: Adoption of strategies

Mind-blowing experiences are major parts of our lives. Therefore, to progress into the next chapter of our life, we need to challenge these experiences and make life an interesting one. If we adopt certain strategies we believe will work in our favour then that is the start of realization of one's self. My adoption strategy is simple and has been used by millions of people who have achieved their dreams knowingly or unknowingly. It basically throws questions at you and waits for answers. Such questions shed light on the problems in your life that need addressing. It could be your career, marriage issues, classroom habits, assignment, work colleagues and so on. In effect, it straightens the path to positive thinking in three basic steps. When in doubt, repeat the whole pattern again until you become used to a set pattern of events. This strategy weans you from your old habits and replaces them with an exceptional character. It ultimately becomes a habit-forming process. But remember that adoption strategies basically entail using the Step 1 approach and the Step 2 approaches, which have had a positive impact in your life. From my experience of this strategy, it involves a cyclic pattern of events. Some of the events are used while some are discarded. It is like a jigsaw which gets turned on and off. The moment a light shines towards a positive change, the subconscious mind get tuned in and triggers a conscious change. This change is, in effect, seen from the behaviour of the individual in question, as is shown in the diagram below.

Self-attainment

The diagram below shows the three steps towards positive thinking.

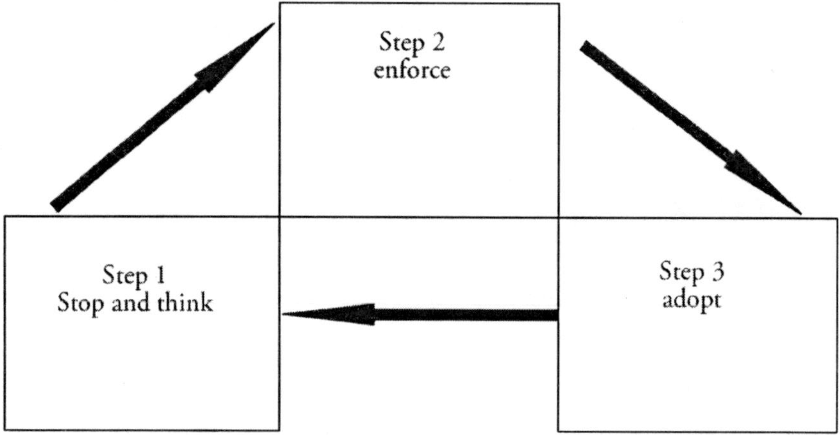

The cyclic pattern of events ensures that at any point or stage in your life you can still achieve a positive effect. If you seem to be drowning your sorrow, you had better wake up and start fighting the just cause. Believe it or not, a place in your heart constantly calls for positive self-attainment. Don't be left out in the process of self-justification and belief. If you believe you are special, then start now to adopt certain strategies that would help you throughout life. These basic steps are principles that will help you towards self-realisation. A stitch in time saves nine. Yes, but don't let the nine become the better part of you. An adoption strategy starts off with a moment of reflection. Believe in yourself and believe in your cause and I can assure you that with divine essence on your side everything else is rest assured. You will definitely become a piece of emulation that stands to test generations to come. Are you ready to embark on this cause? I believe you can do it. Better now than never. I challenge you.

Positive Lessons 2

- Any decision-making process depends on our ability to use the basic things around us to make an informed judgement in our thoughts.
- The ego tree principle could be key to a right decision. The tree here stands for the branches of reasoning; the diversification of man's thought.
- Brainstorming our mind with different information at times could be reasoning behind certain wrong decisions. My advice is 'Stop and think.'
- Risks challenge our ability to reason and determine amongst many those who are willing to take the chance.
- A risk has two sides to it: those who embrace it and the rest that shy away from it. To test your inner self you need to challenge your wits from time to time.
- Outcomes are the very start of any decision-making process.
- For every effort to achieve an objective is worth more than gold in a gold mine. Childhood dreams are mere aspirations.
- The power of positive thinking is beyond limitation.
- Your fate is on your hands. Leave it alone and it will definitely come back to haunt you.
- The gift of understanding is something we have, without which we become victims of our negative thoughts.
- The choices that we have in life are what make life interesting.
- Regrets are there as part of human process, involving our minds: as a reservoir of lessons.
- If I were to speak my mind about life, I would say that our emotional elements could be a step closer to human understanding.

- No thought comes without reasoning; likewise no cause comes without an effect.
- Our expectations in life could be our motivator; our fulfilment, another chapter.
- If destiny still stands in the midst of all eventualities, could I be sending any message of hope? Think again.
- Hope is for those who do understand the ideologies of life.
- How realistic are our goals when it comes to setting them?
- Do not let people in clouds of negativity embrace every facet of your life.
- Do not let uninviting excuses be the cause of your failure.
- Great minds think alike is a saying, but do you know that great thought came from minds like yours?
- If you basically believe you are the epitaph of your existence, then everything can be yours.
- It is up to us: what we do believe? An aspiring mind could be the key to our success.

CHAPTER THREE

Fear of the Unknown

Our fear has not only become one of the greatest obstacles towards self-attainment, but has derailed us from knowing the obvious. Man in himself has thoughts and processes this information as he ploughs along. He has become a victim of fear, but if he consciously decides to align himself with whatever fears that embraces him, that could be a different story. It could be fears from different aspirations to fears of the unknown. The fear of the unknown is human disarray, which basically captivates its victims in all respects and reduces them to a sad and pathetic existence. Man often asks questions on how to get to the next level of attainment even when the odds are against him. The fear of not knowing weighs him down and then he becomes sad and confused.

The way forward now becomes a resistance to progression; fear has now become an idol, which has captivated its victim and has led its victim astray. One of my greatest fears was for my personal achievements.

I used to see things differently, and for me the fear had a strong hold on me. It wasn't just the fear of failure, but the fear of being mocked by society and my peers. The flashes of my wondrous thoughts initiated my determination to succeed, and I usually asked questions like; if I fail, then would it not be a mockery not only to myself, but also to my family that has staked so much for my education? Instinctively, my fear became my drive and that was the story of a young's man dream and fight to survive. As the words of wisdom state, 'fear of God is the beginning of wisdom'. Wisdom is perceived in general as logistic reasoning that supersedes all precepts of failures. To fear God, drives you to walk in the positive paths and when this is achieved; your fears becomes an illusion. Have you thought about this? The start of something familiar brings forth certain fears of the unknown. Even when something is known, the fear of not knowing about it can become the problem. Have you actually sat down and started seeking out your fears? Some fears could be your strength, others your weakness. Have you come to terms with sorting out those fears you know that were there, but turned a blind eye to them? To seek is to believe, as searching could be rewarding. Just don't sit on it and believe everything is going to be all right. I once had this fear of securing admission into university and the fear of how it would all turn out was surrounded by problems like financial crisis and cultural differences. My first hurdle was to believe first that I could do it, and to accomplish this I had to embrace my fears even though I did not know what to believe in. My fear turned out to be my strength through the 'seek and believe' slogan. Since the search for my intuition turned out to be rewarding, I learnt to conquer my fears. This is one of the most educative experiences I have ever had. The ability to know how to defeat your fears lies in your own hands. As mentioned earlier, in chapters 2 and 3, you are the epitaph of your existence. If you want to discover who you are, then start now to defeat your fear.

Have a look at the algorithm below.

Fear of the unknown + other factors ⇒ self attainment +other factors

⇓

Downward slope of self- esteem

⇓

Self pity

⇓

Low crevices of self -pity

⇓

Negative self -attainment

- Depression
- Suicide
- Sadness
- Lost self -identity
- Self denials

From the algorithm of the fear of the unknown, one can see how it can lead to either negative or positive self-attainment, and these are dependent on several factors. The positive sign indicates all motivation factors which feed on the unknown and drives the individual towards achieving goals that are personal. These factors include embracing your fears, reflection moment, power of positive thinking etc. All these have a positive influence on the individual in question. On the other hand, the negative sign include all factors that drive the individual towards losing one's identity in the end. Such factors are many, but we will mention a few: low self-esteem, no reflection moments, living in fear, ungodly practices, no drive in life etc. All these and a lot more will definitely lead to negative self-attainment. If we align ourselves with the environment through reflective episodes of true searches for who we are, we will find so many answers. Those answers that you find most attractive towards rebuilding your low self-esteem could be the start of your journey.

Fear of the unknown sometimes masquerades as failure and is probably one of the most captivating challenges towards removing the shackles of the unknown. Failure is looked upon as the condition of not achieving one's desired end. Consistent failure brings fear and, if failure is marked by fear, then the problem of unravelling the mystery behind our fears becomes an interesting journey; the reason for becoming a non-starter is obviously seen in the eyes of its victims. I remember playing a game once in my school with a friend of mine. It was very tense because we had to bet on sharing our school lunches with whoever won. To my greatest shock, I lost my first bet ever. It was just a game of the ping-pong, but to me it was a challenge. I then, decided to learn certain tricks that he didn't know about and later won a match against him. The trick was obvious: I capitalized on his weakness, which made him lose concentration and in effect I won, not because I did better than he did, but because I knew my strengths and his weakness. I capitalized on his weakness for the sake of winning. The lesson here is: know your strength in order to maximise your potential.

Human life, as it seems, comes with a lot of 'baggage'. If we strive to survive in a world full of unplanned events, disappointments and many more besides, then we ought to start learning from our mistakes and the mistakes of others. Failure is a sad experience, but if you live and learn from it, then the rest of the world is yours.

Only those who consciously understand the elements of life will reap the benefit of life's lessons. The choices that we have among various options can either make us or break us. The question here is, are you on the right path towards making the correct choices or on the wrong terrain? The fear of making choices among various options is the key to our self-attainment.

We have to take necessary measures to ensure that we do have self-control in our life and, to do this, we need to choose the right options as they come our way. When our fears begin to take a hold on every facet of our lives and enslave us, then that is when we need to rise up and say 'no' to it.

A word is enough for the wise, is a brilliant saying; don't keep dwelling in the realm of fear, because it can be misleading in every facet of its comprehension. The ideology here is to embrace your fears and let this become your strength. Self-actualization can only be achieved if the individual in question has forgone all their fears and thrives in the realm of self-control.

Positive Lessons 3

- Most of us have become engulfed by fear of the unknown. Unveil this mask of unhappiness and start living.
- Our fears have become our tears, and our tears a weakening factor. Be careful of your vices.
- Our state of mind ensures we can defeat all obstacles. Challenge your mind at all times and you will be amazed how your mind works.
- Those things that you wouldn't do normally because all your life you have been shackled, start on a day to day basis to tackle these fears.
- Have you allowed time to ask yourself what goes on in your mind during those instances of fear? Use the counteracting attitude to conquer your mind state. For example, fear of driving a car for the first time. Get into the car and drive. The more you drive the more you will conquer your fears.
- Fear of failure is one of the captivating vices of our time. Embrace it and try again. If you fail, there is always a lesson to be learnt from this situation.

- Because most of the time we don't know what the future holds, I advise you to have this outlook on life: life never goes the way we predict but triggers off signals that could lead to a better understanding of it.
- If you search and search and then find, you will understand the meaning of not giving up hope. We are here for one reason, amongst others, and that is to survive.
- The problem at times is the fear of making choices among various options. My advise is, although for any particular decision making that takes place it is quite hard, if you believe you are on the right track then no matter what happens you will definitely learn from it. Fear of the unknown can at times present itself as fear of the known. The truth about the whole scenario is that if we believe in our essence and keep up the good work, we are bound to approach such a concept in a very tactful and thoughtful manner. But remember that the fear of the unknown can at times masquerade as failure.
- We all have fears but the one that matters to us most is the one we constantly come up against. The crux of the matter is; if we shy away from them, it then becomes an increasing problem in our daily lives.
- Your fears could be your weakness and, for you to self-actualize, you need to stay strong and fight your fears. Start a new page and fight this cause that could free you from unnecessary anxiety and depression. My plea is that you decide here and now to change and to work on your fears. Enforce little practical measures in order to conquer your fears.

CHAPTER FOUR

Complexes

Our character comes from our reservoir of memories that have been stored at some point in our lives. The greatest effects on us are the ones that exhibit themselves in the conscious realm. Our character formation comes from our perception of circumstances around us. Those that get expressed are the ones we acknowledge in the physical realm.

Complexes stem from character formation; it could be an inferiority complex or Narcissism or a Napoleon complex. In this chapter, two complexes will be mentioned in detail, inferiority and superiority complex (Narcissism). Individuals have complexes and these are subject to the psyche of the individual in question. Complexes have vast meaning, but the individual normally drives the different complexes in question. Going back to my secondary school days, when bitter competitiveness was a part of me, I found out that there were people who shied away constantly from expressing themselves publicly while others had the nerve to embrace whatever was put before them. In such circumstances, Narcissism has an upper hand in most things and hence excelled in social interactions, while those that hibernated were classed as 'bouquets' in France (mediocre). They weren't called for in times of need and this made matters worse for them, in effect reducing their self-esteem to a minimum (inferiority complex). Even though Narcissism was there at the time of birth, it was probably suppressed as the, so to speak, rennet of other factors. There were others, especially the guy with a 'hunch back'; he generally excelled in academic studies particularly in science subjects. He was smart, believed in his capabilities and constantly gave us a healthy challenge; such a psychological state was classed as a Napoleon complex, which dates back to olden times. A detailed explanation of Napoleon cites the case of scenario handicap, which overcompensates for the victim's state of affairs.

Powerful people at times have complexes, which is based on arrogance. The psyche here probably stems from their well being of 'who they are'. To succeed in life you need to shift from inferiority complex to superiority complex, and to do this, you need to know what phase you are in. Are you in the weak or strong phase? If you are in the weak phase, (inferiority complex) then you need to take positive steps in correcting your complex behaviour.

To shy away from tasks even makes you weaker, but to try and to fail will eventually make you a stronger person. I believe that, as a result of unconvincing excuses in certain men's hearts, masked by the deceptive power of mind, everyone should have a say in these problems. The first port of call is to know who you are. But vital components, which make you who you are, are ascertained by having reflective moments. Are you aware that reversal of success masked by an inferiority complex is one of the challenges facing the 21st century? Personal development is a vital component of this and, in order to eradicate this, we need to integrate positive measures that would suppress such behaviours and express the Narcissism in them. Teach a child and he will learn your ways. The problem is of not knowing is an issue, but, when it is known, the corrective measures to sort out the problem should be put in place. But most of the times it is the problem of not knowing what complex we fit into that destroys the whole ideology.

In the year 2005, I met up with some new people at work, and as we were all staff of the same company we did a lot of things together. In the midst of all this, I noted that one of our staff colleagues had a complex based on inferiority. Most of her answers were 'I cannot', which immediately struck me, as I knew what she was battling with. I later called her, and told her that her greatest weakness was always expressed in these two words, 'I cannot'. I then insisted on giving her some tasks, which she did and she became very pleased with that. A year later, she had the opportunity of becoming an occupational therapist at a highly reputable hospital. She quickly called me and asked for my advice because her mates and others had discouraged her from applying for the position. The first thing I asked her was, 'do you want the job?' She replied, 'Yes, I do want the job.' Immediately I said to her, 'What's stopping you from getting it?' The reply was, 'They said I might not be suitable for the job.' Then, I said to her 'If you honestly believe in yourself and truly want this job, then I challenge you to go in for it.' She was quite happy and she called me a few weeks later requesting that I help her sort out things concerning the job.

In the end, she got the job in occupation therapy and she is now enjoying the moments of her progression from a weak to a strong complex. If we listen to millions of souls out there who constantly undermine our capabilities, not out of jealousy but because they do not understand the importance of being in control of your life, we would definitely stray from our path.

A good complex is a 'superior complex', someone being in control of his life. He dictates what happens and how it happens. He understands that life is full of ups and downs. The ups he embraces, the downs he rejects, but unfailingly learns from this. He is constantly having moments of reflection. On the other hand, the one that wallows in self-pity fails to realize that the society has fallen short of its dignity. In such a scenario, they fall and fall to the depths of 'no return'. As it stands, make sure you don't become a victim of such devastating behaviour – a behaviour that is not called for, swept away by the waves of oblivion and masked by the deceptive power of our psyche. The message is clear: strive to success, fall to rise and shift phases in so-called complexes in order to achieve certain goals that are dear to you. If you seek success that comes from the heart and strive for healthy challenges, then you recognise the need to wake up to this early call and start the 'fight'. Yesterday, which has gone, could have been your day. Let us all make hay while the sun shines, because it could have been the hay that would have made your way. Have a look at the following complexes:

Complex A: Inferior being
Complex B: Superior being
Complex C: Napoleon being

Looking now at this evaluation, how do you rate yourself? Do you believe that a man can at times swing from inferiority to superiority complexes or vice versa? Make a list of the circumstances and events that can actually place you in any of these phases. Take a look at these examples:

- When placed in an unfamiliar situation, what do you do?
- Suppose, suddenly, you found yourself in a situation where you had to act but you shied away.
- Do you feel that you have got any social class?
- Do you always feel you are in lowly position?

These are some of the circumstances that actually make you feel different. So how then do you fit in? The answer basically depends on your approach to life. If you believe in yourself as a superior being, it will eventually unfold as you communicate, stand and socialize. If not, it will definitely affect your performance in any task. This is because doubts will be your greatest fear and, as these occur, you will become anxious, with sweat streaming down by the second. You will find that, all of a sudden, it becomes really overwhelming staying in that situation, so your next approach would be to abandon the situation. If you do, then it means you have succumbed to its boundaries, and in effect lost all self-esteem. My advice would be to fight it both psychologically and physically. Keep reassuring yourself that you can do it, and you will be amazed by your achievements. Align yourself with these situations and you will be amazed how comfortable it can be. Why do we adhere to such practices of imperfection? If we embrace superiority in all its ways and work towards becoming a perfect being without too much pressure on ourselves, we will get there. The principle of 'doing is mastering' could be the key to your understanding. If you complete a task wonderfully well, next time you come across such task it will no longer be a problem to you. It is all about self-belief and challenges in life. Most people that I find very helpful are those who had gone through the same 'bad patches' in life and have got a lot of experiences to share. Those are the ones that boost your self-esteem and place you in a class of its own. Don't neglect who you are. We all have qualities that are unique to us. Find what it is you have and use it as you challenge yourself. It helps towards boosting your personality formation. We do at times stick to practices of imperfection because we feel it is the only way out. But that is not true; rather it is finding excuses for your practice. Avoid it and you will have a clear picture of what you really want. What we want at times will not be what we basically need. 'Want is of the mind but need is of importance' because it basically sustains and makes us feel a lot better no matter what circumstances we find ourselves in, provided we fulfil them.

Complex is a state of the mind, expressed by the victims and pronounced by their observers. If Narcissism is a very crucial part of procreation, then man naturally is classed as a superior 'complex'.

Positive Lessons 4

- Our character formation comes from our perception of circumstances around us.
- Man as things stand is a superior being in the animal kingdom.
- Individuals do have different complexes and these do stem from the psyche of the individual in question.
- There are different forms of complexes that do exist. It is left for us to decide where we fit in.
- To shy away from tasks only makes us even weaker.
- Reversal of success in an individual masked by an inferiority complex is one of the challenges facing the 21st century.
- Teach a child your ways and they will learn from it.
- The problem of not knowing is normally the issue, but when it is known, corrective measures have to be put in place.
- The problem with modern man is the air of negativity, which we all seem to exhibit.
- The problem sometimes with life is that the moment we run into a difficult situation, 9 times out of 10 we turn to the wrong crowd for advice.
- The quest of being in control of your life involves the challenges, which we all undergo throughout life.
- The 'crevices of no return' is a slogan that depicts the struggle of man when he falls beyond the limits of recovery.
- Complex is a state of the mind expressed by their victims and pronounced by their observers.

CHAPTER FIVE

Boundaries of Uncertainty

We are all uncertain about events that are going to happen in the future. Life is full of mysteries and it circles around our boundaries of uncertainty. Even though we are all uncertain about some events in the future, it doesn't necessarily mean we should halt all processes towards knowing who we are. The year 2002 in London was a good and remarkable year for me, which was the year I got my pharmacy degree. Yet, the uncertainty behind my career towards becoming an established pharmacist was the one I could not predict. I knew I had my self-belief and felt the 'divine presence' as always. I sat in my sitting room, dwelling on my thoughts and then it came to me: yes, you are going to be a pharmacist who helps people towards health matters. Then I asked myself what the next step was going to look like. There I sat, confused in my thought, with a series of questions like:

- What is my purpose?
- Why am I breathing with little effort?
- My voice signifies my essence, so where is it coming from?
- I must have a soul, but where is it? What exactly do I believe in?
- Why all these questions?

It was only then that it dawned on me that my existence was for a reason, and that I should use my career to buttress myself and disseminate positivity among men. The fact that I was a pharmacist was a boost to my belief, and then my struggles in life strengthened my character. In effect, I was a whole being, who used nature's gift to strengthen my weaknesses and then, to make them my strengths.

We all have reasons for being here; have you taken time out to find out why you are here? These are basic examples of self-discovery and self-discipline. Man has been born into the struggles of life, which he has been designed for, but has he actually utilized all the elements to maximize his potential? I believe we are still far from maximizing our potentials. As we search and search for answers concerning our existence, it seems to take us in new and different directions. The boundaries of uncertainty coincides with the evolution of the human mind. Questions like, where am I going to be in ten years time, or how will I embrace death? Keep running in our minds.

Take a close look at the following three scenarios and visualize the importance of uncertainty in our lives.

Scenario One: Mr Cox, the accountant at a well-established firm, had realized that he was not financially buoyant. So, he decided to take a few steps towards recovering from his financial problems. Day one came and he opened a savings account. On day two, he finally agreed to decrease his flamboyant lifestyle and settle for a more peaceful life with his family. Finally he became more aware of his spending and was cautious when it involved money matters.

Scenario Two: Emily, the waitress at a local restaurant, could not understand why life had suddenly turned against her. The first month came and it was all about death staring her in the face. Her husband had died in a ghastly motor accident and it was all in the name of seeking wealth. To Emily it was a harsh reality that she didn't know how to manage. To make matters worse, few months later, she received an unwelcome phone call. 'Hello, who is it?' she asked. 'My name is Martins', the caller said, 'and I am calling from a loans company.' She replied, 'How can I help you?' The man now went on to explain how her late husband had borrowed some money from them and hadn't paid it back. On asking the amount, she realized that she was in a major debt, and that was the beginning of her nightmares. She put down the phone and slumped in her chair. To Emily, life was not worth living anymore.

Scenario Three: Take a close look at these events. Vicky was single and had just given birth to a healthy-looking boy. She was pleased with that, but her problem was how she was going to fit in working and looking after her baby. She was only paid a modest wage and from that she had to pay all her bills. The problem started when she couldn't go to work because her boy was ill and she had to look after him. After a time, she was asked to leave because her absence from work kept reoccurring. How then would she cope with all these financial stresses now she was without a job? Think about this.

If you study the three scenarios carefully, it all circles around our boundaries of uncertainty. Mr Cox had to reduce his flamboyant lifestyle in order to accommodate the future. Emily and Vicky have to work really hard to get back to a normal life. If they don't, their lives will become a sad story to those that knew them, and that's not what life is all about. What's going to happen in the near future will be a question that many people may ask.

Our dealings towards achieving our personal dreams all circle around the boundaries of uncertainty. No matter how we see it, we are all tied to these boundaries. But if we have a positive outlook on life and stay on the right path, I believe that our boundaries of uncertainty will begin to unravel as we advance through the endless circumstances of life in general.

Our boundaries of uncertainty could be our fears or our strengths. Just believe in yourself and align yourself with your boundaries and start embracing your blessings as you go along. Don't you know you are a rare gift among millions of people on the planet? No one is as unique as you. If you strive hard in the realms of the boundaries of uncertainty, you could reap the benefits of life's lessons. Strive to become a better person and leave a valuable legacy behind. Your legacy could be a million teachings for the future generation. Don't be left out in the teachings of life, because you could be one of the teachings of an exemplary piece, a moment that deserves emulation, a piece of art that digs deep into the 'essence' of our existence. I believe in the principles of self-teaching and awareness, and whatever you lay down as your core foundation will definitely lead you to eternity. So many people I know, friends, family and colleagues have a basic question, What drives you in life? My answer is: my life. In an explicit sense, my life is the product of obstacles and triumphs, but these I embrace and strive to become an epitaph of my own existence. While others may be amazed about my attitude towards life, that 'aura' basically drives me further into knowing more about human existence. My advice is that you be 'yourself' and work towards becoming a better 'you'. In life, our boundaries could be our strength; it is what you make of life that it turns out to be. See yourself as in the top class of society and you will definitely start to match along the contour of your imagination. Otherwise, you might see yourself as one of the 'drooping dumplings' I have talked about earlier. Be wise about life and make it your bed of positive lessons. We all circle around the contours of our existence; make yours an interesting journey.

Positive Lessons 5

- The 'unknowing world' is full of uncertain events, but with a positive outlook to life you can defeat these obstacles.
- He who understands the concept of life will ultimately begin to reap the rewards of the mysteries surrounding life.
- The psychological implications of uncertainty are many and that is the reason why nature has bridged man's understanding to a point, for example, death at an untimely hour.
- Our essence signifies life, if we believe in ourselves, and then the rest is history.
- We all match along the boundaries of uncertainty, believe it or not.
- 'No one knows tomorrow' is a saying, but if we were to align ourselves with these boundaries then we would have another story to tell.
- Life in itself is made up of boundaries and these are masked by uncertainties; think about it.
- The simple meaning of a question is bound to be an uncertainty. For example, am I who I say I am?
- The reasoning behind an event triggers off the uncertainty of life. Believe it or not, those that foresee these understand the simple meaning of life.
- To my understanding, we are what we are; less understanding and we will be faced with a doubtful future.
- The progression of man looks back at history, but stresses the needs of the future. In between the realms of the past and future lies the uncertainty of life.
- Because we have been created the way we are, it is only left for those who seek out the elements of life to understand its precepts.

CHAPTER SIX

The Ideology of Not Living

Frankly speaking, we live in a world full of people with different backgrounds and cultures. With so much respect for differences that exist, we have patterns in society that enforce living life to the fullest, while other patterns promote a very remote life. From my observation, both are the same depending on what angle one is looking at it from. People believe in what they believe, but when it affects the structure of our society, then we definitely need answers. Some people go through life without having an input into the system. They neglect and abuse the system and call it all sorts of names, while in themselves they have already lost their identity. Such people are normally classed as nonentities of society. The problem here is that most of them lackadaisically attach themselves to the ruins of society and finally embrace self-pity and dejection. Life would basically become a 'dump' if we embraced all the negativity on the planet and masked it with the name of an aimless society. Such a society, when infiltrated with such people, will definitely lead to regression. If a man poses a threat to his surroundings, then he becomes an outcast in relation to it. And if he believes that he has dominion over all things on earth and abuses its course, then that is branded as life not worth living. We are all at some point in our lives not living, but what makes us masters of this universe is when we descend to the realms of this underachievement but try our best to come out and start again. If you live in the ruins of the society and still believe you are on the right track, the question for you is, are you living or not living? There are so many instances of 'not living' that exist in our society. To find out, is to test and see whether your number contributes positively to the society. If you find yourself in the positive phase of life, then I applaud you; otherwise begin with the three step approach in chapter 2.

We believe in the principle of life and its consequences. If you search for 'who' you are and find it, then start enjoying life; otherwise you could remain in the ruins and be lost forever. Any individual who is branded with the slogan 'not living' should strive hard and become one of the fallen men who have risen to become saviours of men. My advice is to transcend to the phase of the living and let old habits get discarded. The ideologies of 'not living' exist among us and determine our contributions towards our society. If you are in the phase of self-actualization, you should have determined in what category you belong. Start now to engage in things that matter and instil a positive attitude in our society. The reasons are simple, and my advice is clear; a society that is full of the 'not living' is practically dead. A dead society has no aim towards achievement and therefore leads nowhere. Are we going to become part of that society that has led to a living-dead society or that part that has to fulfil its duties towards establishing a progressive society? All these are questions you need to ask yourself, which will enhance the realization of 'self'.

Phases of 'not living'can come in the following forms:

(1) The gun cultures
(2) Knife culture
(3) People who drain the system of its wealth

Can you think about any aspect of our society that has led to retrogression? Such individuals have lost any sense of reasoning and have fallen to the 'ruins of the society'. They have become a total menace to its very structure and, as a result, the society is struggling. The ideology that people merely exist is true but, when you analyse the millions of people on the planet that constitute a nuisance to the society, and the consequential damage to its very structure, then it becomes clear why we need to address this issue. If you address the number of people contributing positively to society, you will be surprised how a few members have been working endlessly to ensure that the structure of our society still stands. It is not just talking about it, but organizing ourselves so that we can all work together as one unit.

A classic example would be the rise of knife cultures in our society. The knife has become the weapon of justice to whosoever carries it and also represents a source of protection to them but a threat to others. How can one justify their actions even if it involves vengeance of a relative's death? The so-called knife crime has penetrated the system and has spread like a wave of hope to certain losers. A knife as it stands is a piece of metal, which is used for domestic tasks. I once heard about an incident that took the life of a young child, and it all stemmed from gang wars. Most perpetrators of today are the youths of today. They have lost the reason why they are here and have sold their soul probably to the 'demons of hell'. And as a result of this, they see life a bit differently, . For them it's just one lost soul, but to us that's another life taken from this planet for no just cause. My worries are that they don't know what evil they are dealing with. It might be all about 'clicks' and gang wars, but many of them lose it and then become hooligans of our modern society. I believe they are not only treading on dangerous ground but also investing in negativity. It's only a matter of time and their faces will ultimately embrace their conscience.

Another culture seen here is the so-called drinking culture. Man has become addicted to the bottle to the point where he wholly depends on it. Why have we subjected ourselves to such ridicule? Many of us blame our parents and the society for our habits while we have consciously made that choice. My question usually comes in this fashion: your dad didn't drag you to the shop, buy the drink and forced you to drink it, did he?

The reasons for these bad habits are many. Most of their victims will tell stories of how the world has abandoned them and why their parents have not been there for them. Justification of our habits has become one of the main current setbacks towards our self-discovery. We give reasons for our habits and then expect sympathy. We allow ourselves to become an epitaph of misconduct and still believe everything is going to be all right. Have you heard of this saying: that those who live by the gun will die by the gun? By inference from this saying, it seems also that those who live by the bottle will also die by the bottle. I believe that if someone succumbs to his or her habits, it then becomes some kind of 'worship'. Basically this entails believing in something and dying for it. Therefore, have millions of people become 'bottle worshippers'? It could be answered, as the story unfolds, by those themselves who have fallen prey to the world of alcohol – a substance that has been abused by many and has been synonymously associated with evil, while that is not necessarily the case. People have deviated from the things that matter and have now found that they themselves are struggling in the circles of calamities in their lives. Are they ready to learn from this or are they still the victims of a tale of atrocious circumstances? I believe they can still make a living if they believe in themselves and start weaning themselves off their old habits. This theme is pursued in chapter 17 on old habits die-hard. The ideology that some people are no longer living, but merely existing, is a reality rather than a myth. To stay on course towards self-fulfilment, we need to remind ourselves why we are here and then explore the wonderful characteristics of nature. Nature is beautiful if we embrace its elements and become one unified structure. The best in us is the ultimate 'present' if we find it. Begin to tap or uncover the mysteries that surround man as you embark on this journey. 'Life not worth living' is a farce and should not be the order of the day. My ideology is that of a living being and not one that has decided to exist. Patterns of personality formation make a major contribution towards these victims. Teach your child to learn from good principles and live life by true principles.

Positive Lessons 6

- Understand the pattern of cultures that exist in our society. It could help instil positive values in your life.
- Ensure you apply every principle of good living, which will make for a progressive society.
- Do not constitute a nuisance to the progression of any society. This could cost a lot of lives in the battle towards self-discovery.
- Do not become one of the many who, due to the fact that they did not get involved with social progress, have become fallen men.
- Self-identity is the goal for any human on this planet. Do not lose your identity.
- A retrogressive society is bound to fail at some point. Do not aid retrogressive acts so that you don't become an 'outcast' in your own society.
- If you fail when you embark on life's long lessons, try and try again.
- Self-pity and dejection can only lead to disastrous consequences like depression. Do not involve yourself in such calamities.
- Embrace positivity and all its elements, and then act according to good principles. A society with many vices cannot survive for long. Avoid such precepts and step into the realms of positive struggles.
- If a man poses a threat to his society, then he becomes an outcast from it.
- The ideology that some people merely exist is, hence, a true saying.
- For every wrongdoing of ours, our faces will ultimately meet our conscience at some point.
- Those who live by the bottle could probably die as a result of their vices. Be careful.

CHAPTER SEVEN

Are you satisfied with your life?

We adopt certain strategies in life and to make it worthwhile; some of them are at the prime of our lives, while others are not. Are you willing to let go and start enjoying life? What is it that you want out of life? These are some of the many questions that we ask, but are we willing to explore life to the fullest? We all have events that will inevitably take place in future. Do we believe that we are capable of changing the course of events in our life? We can all be enforcers of our life and determine our destiny. If you failed in the past and are still in the past, then you will definitely need to change your ways. Vast majorities of us drain our sorrows in pints of lager with the sole aim of solving our problems; we walk in the path of alcoholic influence, and believe that all is well. If you take positive steps towards self-actualization, I believe you will definitely attend to your needs. We all have needs, but some needs are more obvious than others, as we in practice see in our everyday lives. These needs could come in the form of love, fulfilment, survival and so on. We talk about being content with what we have: careers, ambitions and so on. But what I have found out is that for most of us, we are not satisfied with our lives and my question is why is this the case?

Most of us follow the bandwagon of the society and sheepishly get consumed by it. By the time we realize our mistakes, it is too late to reveal our gifts. My search for self-fulfilment stems from a lot of questions I used to ask.

- How can I better myself?
- Why can't I progress?
- Why are we always getting it wrong?
- Oh! I think the world has abandoned me. If not, then why am I in this position?
- Is it they or I?
- Am I cursed?

If we keep searching for answers, which we do, why is it so difficult to get them? I am pleased to inform you that life is simple to those who understand the concepts of nature. We do most of the time go against nature and then complain about our selfish acts. People have lost the 'very best' in them and that's the reason why we have to question ourselves from time to time. A common scenario here is what happens all the time in our lives. An individual, talented with 'gifts of the hand', which entails that he is very good when it comes to manual activities -- he could fix household utilities and electrical equipment in the blink of an eye -- had opted to do English at university. My question was, how would he excel in English language when his 'talent' was based on manual skill? I am not saying that English language is not an interesting degree to go for. But when it comes to expressing one's inner self to the fullest, he will definitely have problems. He might score good grades but that will surely not satisfy him when it comes to self-fulfilment. People talk about their wealth, successes and personal achievements but even with these, they are not satisfied with their lives. I sincerely believe that if we as individuals equilibrate with the contours of nature, then our inner self will definitely express itself. But how then, do we equilibrate ourselves with the contours of nature?

The problem here is our modern society. Most of us don't really understand the difference between the concept of our modern society and the concept of nature. Nature ensures we live in equilibrium with each other while that's not the case with our modern society. There are a lot of wars going on and this, in effect, influences the 'average man'. The question now becomes, how then do we embrace nature to unveil the rare gift in us? The answer lies in the hearts of men who seek sincerely for what is theirs. The words of the wise state that gifts are given to men to use them, but if they fail, the gift would be taken away from them and given to others who sincerely seek for it. In order to ascertain our rare gifts and stay satisfied, we need to start understanding the concept of life and its laws. These all coincide with the laws of nature and not of the land, which is man-made. When outlining the laws of nature, there are three in particular you have to pay attention to. These are the laws of cheerful giving, 'the seek and find law' and sacrifice. If you perfect these three laws, you will definitely have unravelled some of the mysteries behind life. To give a gift with your heart adds a lot of meaning to it – I do care for you – and it also sends out the message of love, which ties in with self-sacrifice for another. The problem with society is that man has lost the essence of living and has masked it by the payee system. It literally predicts that for every sacrifice I put myself through, I have to be paid for it. The problem with this is that the society is no longer in unity and this has led to the chapter of love and hate relationships. If you truly love someone, then you must be willing to make sacrifices. I have witnessed a lot of circumstances where two friends had made perfect sacrifices for each other but had used the word 'owe' in return. This basically ensures even though one or the other had sacrificed a lot at one time, he is requesting the other person to pay back the 'borrowed time', which in effect is no longer a 'sacrifice' made. This is basically what our society has become: we get paid for everything we do and as a result lose so much in the course of nature. Nature has its way of doing things so embrace it and learn the obvious. Our conscience can lead us if we listen to her. We do disregard the little voice that advises us from time to time. She constantly voices her opinion, but we defiantly refuse to listen and string along with the crowd. That's why on many occasions people will say, I am contented with what I have. But that's not really the satisfaction I am talking about. When you are contended with what you have, are you satisfied? Definitely not. The only way out is to use the 'seek and find' rule described earlier. The seek and find rule actually ensures that one is actively seeking for ways to improve on certain aspects of one's life. It also means that one is constantly seeking for answers through the reflective moments. I believe if you maximize the use of the three steps towards realistic positive thought, you will definitely have your gifts revealed. The concept to life is quite mysterious and that's one of my challenges. If I were to sum up life, I would say that life is the mystery behind all reasoning. We do reason to believe in what we believe in, i.e. life, but have you asked yourself why life is in continuum with reasoning? If you were to answer this, it would appear that if life had more to it, then that had come with reasoning, and even to appreciate life in itself, that's reasoning in all its ways. Therefore to be satisfied with your life, you would have to embrace the concept of reasoning.

Positive Lessons 7

- Satisfaction with life can only be attained when one's purpose in life is fulfilled.
- The problem I have envisaged is that most of us do not understand the reasons why we are here.
- People should start believing in themselves, which will inevitably help change the course of events in their future.

- Most of us who dwell in the past and see the past as our enemies will never create a successful path towards self-discovery. My advice would be to wake up.
- The vast majority of us drown our sorrows with alcohol, with the sole aim of solving our problems. To me that is just the beginning of another problem in our lives.
- The problem with the common man is the need for something out of reach.
- We do have different categories of friends in life; establishing the ones that are dear to you is of prime importance.
- Always remember, for everything we do in life that is evil there is a repercussion for it.
- A close revelation of ourselves will ultimately stare us in the face at the time of death.
- 'The problem I have with life is we humans.'
- How envious can a man be, even with his pile of wealth, is a destructive characteristic
- To say that we are contented with what we have is an understatement, satisfaction; the ultimate .
- We do have different needs, but those that we come across in our everyday lives are the ones we express.
- Most of us follow the bandwagon of society and sheepishly get consumed by it. Are you one of them? Think.
- We express our intentions from time to time, but do we understand them?
- Nature understands us, but do we understand nature? I believe sometimes we do, others we don't.
- The gifts of nature are given to men to use to effect a positive change in their lives, but the problem seems to stem from our ignorance.
- The payee system of society has destroyed one of the important virtues in life: sacrifice.

CHAPTER EIGHT

Society and Life

The term 'society' was coined in the 15th century and it denotes a group of individuals characterized by a common interest. It could be cultural, scientific, political, religious or for other purposes. Society dates back in time, from the hunter–gatherer bands and tribal societies to complex society. Over time, evolution of cultures has had a profound effect on patterns of community. Our community has become that of a complex society, with culture mixes and religion. Who is the society? It is you and I, and for the society to progress, we need to ensure that we all work strongly towards instilling a strong structured system.

Is the society in itself right or wrong to instil positive attitudes in an individual? It basically depends on what angle you are viewing it from. To reflect on positive attitudes and draw out all the positive thoughts in people, I will view certain negative influences, which the society has on its victims. The main problem here is the so-called 'crowd followers'; many people are stuck in the views of other people. They seem to imbibe those views without harnessing themselves to the important values. It has become the norm of the society because it is what every individual seem to have adopted. They sheepishly join the crowd and fail to realize that, if you are to be in control of your ways, then you need to start looking at different views from a critical angle. I am not attacking the views of many, but I am trying to draw out a positive lesson from this. For illustrative purposes, a man who seeks wealth because he is of the opinion that wealth is all there is in life, will eventually discover that life in general encompasses all things and that wealth in itself is just a proportion of life. If individuals embrace wealth as life, they will definitely succumb to the ruins of wealth. Start now to look for things that matter in your life; it could be your career, your wife, your husband or even having kids. Many of us fall into this category but sometimes we choose the worst in place of the best. It seems that some of us are too lazy to settle for the best. In an attempt to impress, we succumb to the struggles of life, due to lack of strategic management; a cancer that eats away the basic efforts of man. Can't we all see society's baggage and the choices before us? A different message to that would be absorbed by the audiences who have been listening to the media and fallen into a fairy tale world. Believe it or not, the power of the media has shifted our norms to the limits of the 'no return' ideology – a straightjacket most of us have found ourselves in, with illusion attached to it. In an attempt to start thinking again like the youths of our so-called descendants, we have fallen back on the powers of the 'paparazzi'. They have indirectly become the voice of the people whose identities have been tagged as 'non identities'. The effect on society is beginning to show, with individuals not knowing what is right and wrong. How do you train a child to conform to ethics you are not probably certain of? Things that don't matter, in effect, displace organized reasoning. Capital punishment has been abolished, with a more subtle way of punishing; the result is alarming. I believe that we have failed in instilling these moral values in our kids. Consequently, there is gross, widespread moral decadence in our society. The society now responds by punishing these teenagers severely at a later age, and the punishment, I believe, is a bit hard on them. The question is, has the individual in question changed? The answer to this involves a search for reality. If we want our children's development to be precise and progressive, then we need to start dealing with the norms of society, not those of the present, but of the past.

In the olden days, a child's development was the duty of the society; each individual in the organized unit exercised its power and ensured that the child behaved according to certain ideals. This resulted in a child being submissive to his or her parents and also had complementary effects in his or her societal interaction. Such a society was very healthy and life was enjoyable in general. But, as the new society swung into place, we began to lose touch with the things that matter and, in effect, the positive attitudes of our kids have gone down the drain. To inculcate a positive attitude into a child who has never been scolded or punished before poses a threat towards self-attainment. This is because those vices and virtues which he has learnt and what is right and wrong is all mixed up. Some of the wrongs he embraces as rights and vice versa. The only way to tackle this is to instil a positive change in a child when he is in the right phase of life. All I am saying is that if you find yourself in this kind of situation, start now to wean yourself off those old habits that are wrong.

The concept of free spirit has always been there and it dates back a long way. Some people believe they have this free spirit, which drives them to do whatever they like. They play along with the 'so-called' free spirit, not knowing that they are still governed by certain natural laws. If you are in this category of people, you need to answers these questions:

- Why is it that the law of the land still has an effect on you?
- Why are you still being governed by the society in which you belong?

The so-called free spirit cannot operate where there are strong laws, which drive people and ensure that the norms of our society still hold from generation to generation. If you still dwell on those thoughts, then think again: when thunder strikes, we look for answers; if someone dies, we mourn, weep but at the same time mock or reject certain beliefs. If you still insist, then your options of becoming a person who instils positivity in people could be limited. I believe in God, the laws of the land, and I equally believe that if you consciously search your unconscious mind for answers, you could reveal some of the mysteries surrounding life. We live in a world full of different thoughts, ideas and mysteries, but as I searched for identifying the true values in our society, I realise that they have all gone down the pan. My thoughts are of positive values, which have been instilled back in the olden days. But, for our modern values, we have moved towards a generation that has failed to realize our identities, but instead have turned a blind eye to some critical values and, rather, have embraced the so-called modern world beliefs. Look at these questions carefully:

- Are we moving towards self-damnation without knowing?
- Are we purposely allowing ourselves to be bombarded by so-called paparazzi?
- Are we tired of being controlled by ideals and have begun to shy away from things that matter in our society?
- Or are we generally cowards who have fallen victims to our fears?

Take a close look at the society as a whole; there is a mix of culture and religion, as I have stressed earlier. New cultures and religions bring about new ideas and new ways of dealing with situations and circumstances. Some cultures do believe in 'after life' and some don't. But when these people are approached, you will find a positive message, which is, on earth I will live my life to the fullest with a positive attitude, so that, when I die, I will live a peaceful life wherever it may be (after life). Such belief has instilled a positive attitude in these individuals; hence, they will live and influence others. The most important thing is the search for who we are and understanding the things around us. A typical example will be the marching in line of the 'drooping dumplings' as they search for rewards. The point I am making here is, if some of us look for a way of getting money out of our society in one way or the other without making any contribution towards social progress, it is like a leech in a pool of blood. As you leech public funds, your self-esteem reduces gradually to a drastic minimum. With so much help from society, you should not settle for the least among all other alternatives, but the choice is yours.

We can go on and on till the end of the world. But one message is clear: don't let yourself be denied of such happiness as you have in you. Release yourself from the shackles of self-denial and damnation and fight positively towards something great against all odds. Achieving greatness can only come from the minds of positive people who seek self-fulfilment through hard work and dedication.

Our society can be said to be stupid, not encouraging but at the same time very caring. As an illustration; let us look at children in school; with no stringent punishments anymore, they live in the realms of 'I do what I like'. As the years pass by, it becomes part of them as they indulge in all kinds of indiscriminate acts. Then, later in their lives when they commit an offence, they receive punishment from our society. These problems in the first place should not have arisen, had these children been given the right direction while they were still young .You can see why society is not very encouraging and at the time stupid. Why can't we all become 'neighbours' of each other and strive towards correcting these vices? Parents, be careful, because according to book of Sirac 30, it states that he who spoils his son will have wounds to bandage at old age and will quake inwardly at every outcry. Parents, be careful how you raise your children so that you don't become the victims of a fallen child.

The Legal System and Responsibility

Man as a being has got his 'thinking cap' on, but when he feels or decides to disregard the laws of the land and do as he pleases, our legal system reminds him that our society has rules that we all have to conform to. The legal system is tightly controlled, with the police, magistrates and lawyers all working hand in hand to ensure that these rules are obeyed. The general message is for you to be aware of the law, as new laws tend to emanate in countless numbers. As a citizen of a country you do have your rights, yes you do, but that doesn't give you the right to do as you wish. For an organized system to flourish, the laws must be adhered to. The problem with our modern society is that we have shifted so much responsibility to the legal system, to the point where they are being overworked as a result of our lack of responsibility. If you ask me, I would say that responsibility is a part of learning and, if we as parents don't teach our children the rights and wrongs, how then do they become responsible citizens of the country? There have been many controversial debates on teacher-parent relationships. As the days go by, parents are becoming overwhelmed by societal influences and by so-called lawsuits that they themselves have become a threat to the educational system. Most parents these days have forgotten the reasons why a child should attend an educational establishment.

A school is a place where a child is taught how to behave and also how to respond to academic matters. It basically involves an active learning process and this leads the child through life. If this circle is broken, then the child will definitely have a lot of problems in life. From my observations, most parents quickly blame teachers for their children's wrongdoings, without questioning their kids in the first place. They sincerely believe they are protecting their own, without realizing that the more they embrace that kind of behaviour the more the child's personality begins to dwindle. At a certain point, a child's self esteem will be highly influenced by his parents.

He will became a man whose ability to make decisions has been stolen from him. He then becomes attached to his Mum's apron strings. Such a man will find it difficult to self-realize because he will always be in doubt when it comes to his capabilities. The ability to make decisions and stand by them is what our nation needs. On the other hand, a teacher knows his or her duties: abiding by the laws ensures that the teacher instils positivity in her students. What would it be like if they were stripped of the right to punish students at school? The answer could be a rise in moral decadence in our society. For teachers to excel in their job, I believe the system should entrust more responsibility to them, because the way the society is going would definitely lead to a society full of misconceptions. Remember, society comprises you and me; so don't get confused when matters like this are being thrown at you. Parents, please embrace your children as your responsibility, and stop embracing and creating unnecessary pressures for our judicial and educational systems. For parents that are in the right phase of life, keep up the good work. There is nothing like reaping the rewards of the good seeds you have sown. There is a saying about parents who have left their responsibility and have shifted it elsewhere. It states that their sons and daughters will become a thorn in their flesh in old age. Don't go about trying to confuse people, while in your own domain nothing seems right! If you look closely at the educational system, it strictly divides the system, based on primary, secondary and tertiary institutions. The problem here is that some of the students in primary schools have already been psychologically defeated when it comes to challenges in life. This stems from the fact that they had been informed in certain institutions that they were not to be classed as grade A students but rather as grade C students. The point is the grade systems should be reviewed, because if we continue like this, most of our youth of today will come out from our academic institution with their 'heads down'.

I have a friend who once told me about his experience in school with his teacher. He was told that he would never make an A and that he was a grade C student. He told his teacher that he wasn't a grade C student and that it was only a matter of time and the truth would be revealed. The scenario here is that all students are grade A students, but it depends on the time to get to that point that matters. Yes, our system may not have the time to groom a child into becoming a grade A if they are slow at assimilating information. This is where parents have to come in and do the extra work needed to guide the students. Are parents willing to go through the courses with their kids at home? This is another theme to ponder. It doesn't seem easy to attend to such responsibilities, but I have witnessed parents resigning from their jobs just to attend to their children's needs. It is a big sacrifice, if I may say so. Education does not only involve academic matters but also involves instilling positivity in a child. Remember, the youths of today will be prime ministers of tomorrow. Are we prepared to fight this cause towards self-fulfilment and justification?

Blame Culture Estranged

Man has become a victim of the so-called blame disease, which infects its victims every millisecond as we breathe. But why have we become subject to this infectious plague that has defeated man's will to fight the 'just course'? We have withdrawn into ourselves with no fight left in us. This institution of blame has led men astray, with millions of souls struggling to get their identities back. For instance, I had this striking conversation with one of my friends about kids' attitude to life. It was a subject of a wrong attitude to life, with blame culture rearing its ugly heads as we conversed. My friend who is currently a teacher, went on to say that the youths of today did not seem to understand the meaning of responsibility and life. They seem to throw most of the blame onto their teachers and in the course of things lose their self-identities. One of his students, on questioning, slandered the teachers and constantly repeated that they weren't there for him. As the questioning went on, the student confessed he wasn't interested in the career concept and that it was better for him if he left the educational system entirely. My friend was shocked, because he felt the student had the wrong attitude towards life and using blame, as an escape route for his mishaps was not the right thing to do. He approached the student and gave him a positive message of hope and advised him on the things he had neglected as a student. Finally, the student apologised for his wrong choice of words.

Why did I bring this example to light? It shows how we respond very quickly when it comes to shifting our responsibility to others. We lost our professionalism a long time ago. Why is this the case? I believe that our society has moved away from its role and has shifted its responsibility elsewhere. As mentioned earlier, a teacher at school has no right to impose very strict punishments on kids anymore and, as a result, these kids have lost their respect for their teachers. Extrapolating from this, it would seem that society has pushed the teachers into a corner and has stripped them of their sense of belonging. This has resulted in a clash of words as parents blame teachers and vice versa. It has turned out to be a circle of blame. If you find yourself in one of these circles, then my advice would be to examine your ideologies of life. Such deceptive powers of the mind delude you from recognizing the norms of the society and have clouded your sense of reasoning. If you believe in the institution of professionalism then you have to start accepting responsibility for your actions. Don't shield yourself from responsibilities and then believe you will enjoy the successes of life. People who shy away from their responsibilities are people of low esteem. In that respect, begin to wean yourself off this concept and start identifying areas you can strengthen to become a responsible being. The problem is that some of us do accept responsibility at times but get shamed and even banished for our wrongdoings. We all make mistakes in our lives, and the sooner we accept them and start working towards achieving personal goals the better for all of us.

Here is an exemplary masterpiece of the depth of blame culture. One of my colleagues at work was sobbing her eyes out when she approached me. I couldn't understand her grief at that instant until she let the cat out of the bag. She said her son had been severely punished for something he admitted he had done, whilst one of his friends who was involved in scratching someone's car had been let off without a charge. He had told a pack of lies on being questioned and his parents had proudly embraced him as their son. My question is, how then do you train a child and instil positive attitude in them while all around them are lies and deceit? If we believe in the principles of understanding life, then such an act would be condemned in every way. Rather than cultivating a habit of self-discipline and professionalism, we have accepted blame and its elements. Blame as the word stands does not promote professionalism; therefore, if you feel you belong to this circle, then look at the following questions carefully.

- Do you put your responsibility onto someone else?
- Do you accept that blame culture has become a better part of us?
- Are you scared you could lose everything, just for accepting your mistakes?
- Do you believe the society has changed for the worse when it comes to accepting responsibility?
- Do you accept dignity and all its elements?
- Are you willing to accept blame, shame the blame and become dignified?

If you find yourself in this circle of blame, as we mentioned earlier, that will be a start to recognizing an important factor in unlocking your precious gifts. If you critically examine the saying 'To err is human, to forgive is divine', life would definitely be viewed from a different angle. Since there is a divine essence attached to forgiving, let us not become fools but rather wise men at heart. Your destiny lies in your actions; safeguard it. As to the legal system and responsibility, man as a being has got his thinking cap on but when he feels or decides to disregard the laws of the land and do as he pleases, our legal system now reminds him that our society has rules that we all have to conform to.

Learn to live and live with principles that matter. As of now, we live in the realms or shadows of the past.

Positive Lessons 8

- If you haven't a mind of your own, and seem to base your decisions on other people, I believe you are a crowd follower. *Advice: Begin to trust your own instincts when it comes to decision-making.
- Life encompasses wealth; wealth is just a minute proportion of the elements of life.
- People who embrace wealth as life would definitely be consumed by its consequences.
- 'Media hype' has become one of the most influential and also destructive characteristics of the 21st century. Be careful of what you bombard your mind with.
- Stringent rules in schools have become a mockery in the eyes of our youth. Have we actually got what it takes to force the societal ideals on these youths? I believe we do, but certain factors as have been mentioned seem to be a problem.

- Moral decadence has been camouflaged as a common joke in society, for example the use of swearwords.
- As a reflective issue, think of the ideals of the past and compare them to the present. What do you think?
- The development of a child's moral, social and physical aspects do not only rest on the parents but on society as well.
- The loss of respect for the planet has been blamed on societal influences, 'the modern society'.
- The things that matter in our lives have been blown away and replaced with artificial things. We seek wealth and career jobs, but the one thing that we did have we have lost – 'conscience'.
- The air of negativity around our youth is increasing at a fast rate. Be careful how you bring up your kids.
- Free-range spirits: these people cannot operate where there is a stringent law.
- The march of the 'drooping dumplings' as they march towards the 'abyss of no return'. This depicts people who merely exist.• Our society can be said to be stupid, not encouraging but at the same time very caring.
- We should become 'neighbours of each other' in order to correct the illusions in our society.

CHAPTER NINE

The Crossroads Analogy

Our journey towards self-fulfilment and justification does not come to an end on this planet; this is because humans are always seeking for a better understanding. In the search for this, man finds himself entangled with his quest for life. If we all are running this race together, why is it that some people get there early while others arrive late? We are what we are, and among many others lies the concealed truth. During my youthful days, amongst my close friends were all a battle of who will succeed the most, and the truth behind this would be revealed. It was after our university careers were over that the sequence of events started to take place. In a blink of an eye, one of my friends got a good job and got married within the same year. He then progressed into having two kids, which was not the end; he further established a company, which he managed. It was only in the latter part of the 7th year that he suddenly kicked the bucket. Death had arrived at his door. It was a shock to all, because we couldn't explain how or why he went from a mediocre to an influential person and died in the midst of it all. To me, it was a life lesson: we did not start this journey together; some start late and some start early. We never know what is round the corner, so we should take every opportunity that knocks at our door, but we have to be wise in making our decisions. The moral lesson views this as a journey of life based on circumstances and destiny. He might have seen a lot of crossroads as he envisaged success but that didn't stop him. He went on and on until he finally gave in to the summons of nature. My question is; have you reached your crossroads? The point is, we all have reached some crossroads to get to where we are now, but this will take us either to the path of damnation or self-actualization. There are many uncertainties that embrace us on our journey in life. Are we prepared to face such issues as untimely death? My own understanding about life is simple; understanding the principles of life is the key to foreseeing our crossroads. Therefore, wherever you are, whatever you do, you are bound to meet crossroads, which will lead you to self-attainment or self-denial. Strive to be the best among the rest, and you will be satisfied with your life. A life viewed as satisfied is worth going for, start your journey gradually and meet it at its end. Our crossroads is the road to our success; make it your choice.

Le carrefour est là pour nous pour changer nos vies effacements (Crossroads are there for us to effectively change our lives). But my question is, what actually put these situations in our path? Life has a way of straightening our path and in effect understands us. Most of the time we try out different things all in the name of getting adventurous and what normally happens is that we become consumed by our ways. These ways may not necessarily instil positivity in us, but rather could destroy our will to succeed. I have this example of how a man embraced death because of the way of life he had chosen. If he had listened to himself, he would probably have recognized his crossroad, but rather he refused to accept nature's warning signs and had encountered death in a nasty way. I heard of this boy who was a student at one of the universities at the time. He was handsome and was very popular amongst students. His Dad was a rich man and in the midst of all this, sent out the message of 'I do have money' as his anthem. Invariably it backfired, because his son became a 'party animal'. One of these incidents happened on his way to a party, which ended up in an accident. It was a fatal one, in which he was the only one that had a lucky escape. He thanked God for that and organized a thanksgiving for himself, inviting everyone. Two weeks later, after the first incident, he was coming back from a friend's party when a second accident happened. This time, he was the only one to die in the accident. Now, the question was, didn't he understand the signs that were being cast at him or did he foolishly throw away his life? From that, you can see how nature, against all odds, still looks after us. But if we choose not to accept the obvious truth, then we are bound to fall, just as trees flourish during the summer and spring and then lose their beauty during winter. That is how man can attend to his needs from time to time. Sometimes, he defeats the obstacles and sometimes he accepts them, learns from them and then moves on. If you try to analyse what drives men to their crossroads, it then makes sense why every being on the planet has a purpose. Most of us deviate from our purpose, and it is a way to say 'stop and think'. Most turning points are there to stimulate us mentally. They are very hard on us; this is because it is probably the last option left to us to effect a change for the better. Most of the times when we embrace such situations we ask why it happened to us, but the simple truth is that we have been ploughing the wrong furrow for a long time. It then becomes our way. Even when we are corrected about our ways, we argue it out and claim we are still on the right path. It is obvious as humans why we try to convince ourselves that we are doing the right thing. It all stares us in the face at the crossroads. So what happens at the crossroads? I would say that if reality hadn't embraced us at some point in our lives, then at the crossroads we would see life as it is.

The painful truth is that at the crossroads life could change forever, but on a close observation, that is one of the realities of life. A classical example of a turning point concerns a woman who disobeyed her husband to travel to another town, in a defiant attitude, only to find herself in an accident that maimed her for life. As long as she lives, she will remember that day she disobeyed her husband and this, in effect, would certainly have changed her ways. But my question is; why do we live our lives the way we do and, even when we embrace reality, at times we still don't listen to its signs? Human beings have the free will to do what they like at times, but when we begin to stray from our path, life tells us that we have rules and that we need to conform to those rules. In effect, if we do want to understand the concept of self-fulfilment, I believe we should do the right thing. So, as you can see, we do need crossroads in our lives to correct our ways when all the signals and revelations have been disregarded. But beyond the crossroads, what do we, as humans, think could be the end result? If we believe in life principles, then we are bound to understand life precepts. Our destiny lies in our actions, as I have already stated, but if we as humans do not understand the warning signs around us, then we are bound to face a crisis of an unforgiving dilemma. The road that leads to a crossroad is the one you need to reconsider, because it can lead you to an ever-increasing quest of bountiful adventures. The road to success is never easy, but if we took the easier option in life all the time, then we would never reveal the best in us. We are not here for games but rather we are here for a worthy purpose, which I believe, is a reflection of our existence.

The ideology here is that at the crossroads, we would embrace a brainstorming session of choices, and it is only those who learn from this that will embrace self-gratification. I believe that every reason comes with a thought and every situation comes with reasoning behind it. Life is full of untold lessons, it is true, but it is only the few who understand this and walk in the path of positive lessons will enjoy the 'elements' of life.

Crossroads and options go hand in hand, but at your crossroads, you will definitely be assured that it is a path for you.

Positive Lessons 9

- Man's justification and self-fulfilment do not end on this planet. This is due to the fact that man is ever seeking more understanding.
- Men do run different races on the planet, so please ensure you stay on your course. * Note: 'we are what we are' is true; truth is concealed amongst the many lies.
- We all do meet crossroads at some point in our lives. The ones who make the right decisions stay on course; others might keep going round in circles.
- Always strive to be the best amongst the rest.
- A life viewed as 'satisfied' is worth going for.
- Crossroads initiates certain thoughts that weren't there initially, and for us to make a choice amongst many options, we need to know where we stand in terms of our goal.
- At a crossroad, we are brainstormed with a lot of information; it becomes a reality check in terms of defining our edge of reasoning. The ones who avoid decision-making get caught up by these situations.
- The path that leads you to that crossroads is the path to your destiny. Be careful how you approach that journey of life.
- Many of us find ourselves overwhelmed with options, but if you really search for true answers, it is always the path with least worries that we humans normally embrace.

CHAPTER TEN

Perception of Health – a prerequisite for a successful career

Health is defined as the sum total of the physical, social and emotional well being of the individual. Health is one of the topics people perceive as boring, but do you know that your health determines your life? Many a times I ask myself, why have humans neglected their health? The simple answer is that we forget to do the things that matter and give excuses as reasons. For instance, if I have a pain, the first option would be to take painkillers. But have I found out why the pain had occurred in the first place? No! This is because we synonymously associate pain with painkillers, and that's wrong. Our attitude towards health has left millions of people unhappy. An unhappy man cannot concentrate on his work, and you can see why most of us fall into this category, and if we don't get out of this cycle, we are bound to pay a very heavy price. We have to make sure that we take good care of our physical, social and emotional well being for us to be happy. If a man neglects this vital ingredient in life, then he is heading for a total disaster. It is not surprising to note that a negative answer is always received when you inquire from people how often they go for health checks. Man has gone a long way towards recognizing his own needs, but to him, health does not seem to matter except when it bites. Why do we leave ourselves to pay a price that is so costly? We go to hospital only when we are sick, only to find that our body seems to be struggling because of our ignorance. When we are happy, our body cells vibrate with joy the reverse is the case whenever we are sad. The model below depicts how the body cells make up a whole being; if part of it is affected then the whole being is also affected. A happy man is a reasonable candidate who ensures that his healthcare needs are met.

Body cells → growth → whole being
↓
Psyche of individual

Model (I) depicts the effect of body cells on the psyche of the individual

If a man is made up of body cells, then he must take care of them, for a decision maker can only work at his best if his whole being is functioning well. When you are sad, it must certainly affect your work. Happiness and health are inseparable; man has to make careful decisions on how to make his journey in life. If you are calm, at peace, loved and happy amongst others, then you are in the right direction for self -actualisation. One needs to avoid the devastating effects of hatred, misdirection, confusion, sadness etc. Positivity is synonymous with success, just as health is synonymous with success. Wrong attitudes towards your health can only lead to destruction. If you are aspiring to become an influential person, and you can't take care of your needs, then you are taking off in the wrong direction. It goes to show that we are sending out the wrong message to others. The problem is that we constantly shy away from our responsibility and blame others. This 'blame culture' has become a major part of our society; for example, a vast majority of us at some point in our lives have blamed healthcare professionals for things that should have been blamed on others. The point is that we normally shift our responsibility to someone else and devise a way of blaming him or her. When things go wrong, it is advisable for us to start checking the functioning of our body, including the heart, kidneys and lungs. It is important to check your cholesterol level, blood pressure, sugar level and so on, and then consult an expert if in doubt. It is good to avoid being caught up by the so-called 'blame culture'. Be a man of wisdom and start sorting out your own health care needs. Your health is in your hands; if you ignore it, it will definitely find you out. Think of millions of people suffering from stresses and all other emotional diseases. They do so because they ignored taking care of their health needs. They wander aimlessly in search for who they are, while a common plague is slowly consuming them. If you are successful and work under stress, these are questions you can ask yourself:

- What causes your stress level to rise?
- Can you avoid this?

Check out some answers below:

- It is your obligation to trace the cause of your stress.
- Yes, you can avoid it, if the cause is detected.
- Set out a realistic target every week to help you avoid your stress.
- Monitor your blood pressure regularly.
- If you are always sad, find ways of becoming happy. Everyone is responsible for his or her own health, so be careful with your whole being, because if you don't take good care of it, it is bound to crash at some point.

If a man is constantly seeking ways to succeed, he must take good care of his whole being. Our body ticks like a clock in response to our activities, which invariably depends on the body function. It is therefore wise for us to avoid accumulating stresses in our bodies, because it counts towards our life span: the more the stress, the less the life span. How then do we maximize our potentials in the mist of all this? The answer is; safe guard your health. Even amongst the elites, health care need is taken as secondary rather than primary. The reasons why we neglect our healthcare are many; but remember that 'a car without an engine is just a piece of metal'. Man can only enjoy the fruits of the land if he invests daily in his healthcare needs. If you invest now, it will go a long way in the future. Don't be like seeds that were lost by the wayside. Do not, because of other needs in life, neglect your health, for if your health collapses, your future is at stake, so do the utmost to secure your health and maximize your potential.

The practicality of life has swayed us from the basics and, as a result, we forget to do the obvious things at times. If I ask one or two people how their body system works, most people will tell you, 'I am not sure.' The reason for this is simple: if you do not look after your body as a whole, then there are bound to be problems, and when they arise you will be confused because you haven't done your homework at all.

I will give you an example. When I was in primary school I had this fair sized wound in my leg. I decided not to attend to it and, few weeks later, I discovered this huge lump around the groin area. To me it was a disaster because I felt something terrible was going to happen to me. It was only when I approached my Dad about my wound, that he explained to me the reasons behind the lump. It was my immune system alerting me that the wound had been infected. So it was a matter of urgency on my part to get the wound treated as quickly as possible. It shows you how we neglect our body system at times. As I have said earlier, know your body and sort out your body's needs. Don't let them harm you before you arrest the situation. Use the principle of my health first before anything else.

One of the things we underestimate that is of importance is what we eat. If you have actually seen the programme on the TV *You are what you eat*, then you will realize how the body system utilizes what we ingest to repair or nourish the body cells. The problem with us is that, as a result of our daily living, we have embarked on high fatty meals to the point where our bodies are suffocating in the midst of its 'own space'. As this happens, the normal biochemistry in the body is impaired and this can result in a lot of diseases. The problem with a lot of people is that they turn a blind eye to it, not realizing it could be the cause of some of their problems. My advice is to at least eat a healthy meal once a day, watch what you eat and safeguard yourself from the dangers of 'house arrest'. What do I mean? There are many problems or health issues, which dramatize themselves without giving you warning. Such health disasters like blood pressure surges, strokes and heart attacks could strike you at any point in time without your attending to them. They could prevent you from achieving your dreams if you don't take the necessary measures now. One of the predominating problems I have envisaged in the search for who we are includes indulging in excesses. When we do things and do them in an excess fashion, they will only come back to haunt us. For example, drinking too much alcohol in a day or working excessively hard to the point where your stress levels are at a peak, will, as I have mentioned earlier, challenge your health. If necessary, avoid the circle of friends who might have aided your addiction.

I will use this opportunity to explain how I instil calmness in my working hours. First, I always remind myself at any point in time, no matter the situation, to embrace a calm approach and, to this day, I have noticed it helps a lot with your reasoning. I see a lot of my colleagues asking me questions on how I stay calm. The point is, discipline helps, but, at the same time, for you to embrace any facet of life with proper reasoning, you have to constantly talk to yourself and remind yourself of the dangers of doing the opposite. And that has actually helped me to stay on course. Calmness comes from the heart, but doing the right thing at the right time helps settle unnecessary agitations. Don't make hasty decisions, because they will only agitate you when you're working. Take a stepwise approach to educate yourself on becoming a better person. Avoid confrontation and seek positive answers to every situation. Worrying has been put in place for a reason, but when we feed on it constantly, it then becomes a problem. I believe that if there is a worry then it means we have to sort out the cause. The problem we sometimes have is that we basically leave the cause and then dwell in the spheres of worry only to later find out that we could have sorted out the cause in the first place.

Most of us exist in this situation most of the time and find ourselves aging very quickly. My advice would be, any time you worry, pick up a mirror and see the effect you are physically having on your system. I am not going to give details of what happens to your inner-self, but you can envisage the alterations in your body chemistry. But the message we are sending out is that it is of a catastrophic nature to dwell in these circumstances. Always smile to keep your system relaxed and in control. A tense face does not make us happy but rather kills our self-esteem. There are so many reasons why we should put on a happy face at all times. The beauty of a smile is unquestionable. It attracts different personalities and makes you an approachable 'human'. It brings out the best in you and nourishes your body cells and gives everyone around you the impression you're a nice 'fellow'.

The list is not exhaustive, but remember, a million smiles out there is worth more than a diamond. Imagine being in a world with only smiles around you. That would be considered a perfect world even though we are far from it. But it seems quite strange why we all present this serious look and brand it maturity. All around you should instil positivity and enhance human relationships. As I have mentioned earlier, the

reason why we are here together is to enjoy each other's company. Such associations are healthy and promote long life and happiness. The perfect orientation for a healthy lifestyle is the organization of the mind. Are you organized mentally or do you just go with what's happening around you?

Positive Lessons 10

- Health is not just about ill-health, but it's all about looking after the whole being.
- Man for some reason has neglected the things that matter to him most, health being a classical example.
- If a man neglects the vital ingredient of life (health) then he is heading for a total disaster.
- A happy man is a reliable candidate who ensures that his healthcare needs are met.
- Health checks are important, but to the average man the cost seems to be the problem.
- Happiness does rejuvenate body cells and this needs to be established in the life of everyone.
- If positivity is synonymous with success then health is synonymous with success.
- Your health is in your hands. Forsake it and it will definitely haunt you.
- The price we have decided to pay due to our modern way of living has scarred our health. * Lesson: monitor your stress levels.
- Please do look after No.1, as your health determines your life.
- Our body ticks like a clock; it counts the miles of stress as you go on the endless journey.
- The common man has branded healthcare as second class.
- Please don't forget the basic needs of our existence. Note: a car without an engine becomes just a piece of metal.
- Daily investments in our healthcare needs will definitely play a positive part in our lives.

CHAPTER ELEVEN

Success can be achieved

Success in any sphere of life can be fulfilling once achieved. My view of success stems from the fact that many of us associate success with wealth, but that is incorrect. The number of cars you own or the stacks of money in your bank does not measure success; rather it is the sense of personal achievements that has been gained through dedication and hard work.

I have mentioned that success goes hand in hand with personal achievement, which is dear to us. I once said to a friend of mine, 'We all talk about success but I believe that if I made a conscious decision to save up £5.00 every day for an item I desperately need and I finally bought that item after I had had a long wait, that says a lot about me and also tells you about the whole journey of perseverance. ' To me that is success; it doesn't have to be huge for it to be acknowledged as success. I have used this example to buttress the fact that success can be looked at from that angle. We all have ambitions, but I have envisaged that one of the reasons why we fail at times is that our capabilities are limited if our will to succeed becomes the pending problem. Most of us fall into this sphere of life. We do not understand the elements of willpower and finally get consumed or distracted by it. One thing I always remind myself is that if my will to succeed becomes the impending problem, then I must ensure that my 'willpower becomes my strength'. So, we have to make a conscious effort to ensure we understand the concept. To take an example, when I was in pharmacy school, I had this friend I met on the second day of school. He was a very nice fellow and had the charm and charisma of a very confident person. But he had a problem with his academic pursuits and when I approached him on this very subject he confessed that even though he really wanted to study pharmacy, he had a lot of distractions. Those distractions finally lead to his downfall and in effect tarnished his will to succeed. He had become a victim of those circumstances, which deter us from our goals. He was a lesson to all those who entered pharmacy school at that session. To this, I would say that if the will to succeed seems to be the problem then your anthem should be practice, practice and more practice!

Most of us forget the time and planning needed to ensure that we become successful in whatever we do. We neglect the fact that for every time spent and spent well, we are bound to gain from it. Most of the times when we are fully engaged in whatever situations we find ourselves, we fail to realize that the more you invest in any endeavour, the more you get something out of it. It doesn't have to be great, but it could lead to other avenues that can help you excel in your work. My close friend was very unacquainted with using computers. It so happened that music was his passion, so he decided to buy some music programs so that he could create some instrumentals for his songs. During the process of creating his instrumentals he mastered how to use computers, and to this very day talks about it from time to time. I can't tell you how amazed I was, but it only sent out a positive lesson, and that is, for anything you do, you need devotion and perseverance for you to excel in that venture.

Man sees himself in different ways, but one of the qualities that embraces him most is his ambition. We do have the urge to be ambitious, but it depends on the individual in question. Many of us join the crowd in things that matter to us, but it is wrong for us to do this. For every being, the course of your journey has been mapped out for you. It is left to you to redesign the path you will like to take. I remember the good old days when I was in seminary school; this is a place where the Roman Catholic priests are trained before their ordination. My ideology was to get in there and become a real person and see what comes out of it. After my three years in seminary school I decided to quit because I knew it wasn't my vocation. I made a conscious decision to leave, since it wasn't my path. My pathway was to get married, have kids and take care of them. But, to my utter amazement, I one day bumped into one of my old mates from the seminary school. It was shocking to see that all those positive attributes we had all learnt in school were 'out of the window'. It was an eye-opener to see people who you really looked up to that had strayed from the right path. The real issue here is that the society in itself passes its negativity among us like waves in the sea. Be careful whom you go with, be wise how you go about things, don't let society's ill effects affect your sense of reasoning. Always remember to listen to yourself when you feel something has gone wrong. Remember, we all circle around the boundaries of our uncertainty. For every ambition, career or even project being considered, there is always an uncertainty that is attached to it. The point is that those boundaries of uncertainty strengthen our character, providing us with a sense of reasoning, which helps us towards personality formation. Success circles around these boundaries and unless you start to address issues relating to your needs, you will never become a better person. Most of us find it very hard to project our future due to lack of reasoning. We live without putting any thought to anything. How do you become an exemplary individual that instigates positivity among men when you are lost in your own world? To incite positivity among men you need to pay a price of sacrifice, hard work and dedication. I remember the story of two families that were ultimately faced with the struggles of life. One family decided to dedicate time to their children and directed them to become educated individuals. The other family coped with life but did not consider training their children as they were engaged with everyday life. The first family progressed into producing excellent kids with positive attitudes while the other family struggled to no avail. It was in the course of discussion that the family who had neglected their duties realized their mistakes and decided to give their kids the education they needed. Everything comes down to sacrifice when a reward is needed. The other family realized that they had to sacrifice their time and leisure hours to inculcate discipline as well as study habits in their own children. Whatever situations you find yourselves in, there is a way out. The possibility of determining who you are is endless, but requires your self-belief.

In life, to get to any point, needs a first step. The question is, how do you go about it? For example, if you want to become an engineer, you ought to start acquiring the basic skills, which you need and this takes time. It then becomes a habit, which you have mastered. This now leads you to challenge yourself to attain new heights. All you need is the firsts step towards self-realization. The more you search, the more you feel your way along your path. Stay on that positive path and be successful. It is not by magic that Jeffrey Archer became one of the most influential people when it comes to writing novels. It is a matter of dedication, interest and hard work. Start now to invest in your future, because every step towards investment in your future goes a long way. Be courageous and face your fears. You don't have to die many times before you're victorious in your field, but if you did and become an influential person, then that is a remarkable achievement.

Success at any level of life can be achieved, provided the person in question is willing to give it all they can to attain the very best out of what is there.

Remember, don't succumb to the 'ruins of success' when you get there. Believe in yourself and align yourself with life. I believe in myself. What do you believe in? The option is yours.

Positive Lessons 11

- Success is not measured by the stacks of money in your bank or the amount of cars you have, but by your personal achievements, which varies with what is desired by the person in question.
- Man's ambition says a lot about him. But if his willpower to succeed undermines his capabilities, that might be his greatest enemy.
- For every individual, the course of your journey has been laid out; it is left for you to redesign the path you want to follow. *This is one of the elements of willpower.
- Success circles around the boundaries of uncertainty, but remember that these events strengthen our character and provide us with some reasoning about certain precepts.
- Sacrifice, hard work and dedication are the three centres of focus for every self-actualizing individual.
- Attainment of self-discovery can only take place if the essence of man's existence is ascertained.
- Take time to learn from your mistakes because they could be the secrets to unlocking the doors to success.
- Be a master in attending to your daily needs. It is all about practice, practice, practice.
- A healthy person is a happy one. A happy one is able to make choices among many options. *A sad person normally has his mind clouded with negativity.
- The possibilities to self-discovery are endless, but depend on the individual in question.
- Ensure at all times that you set a realistic target. This is one of the downfalls of the common man. *The common man normally foresees things unrealistcally, 'an absolute dreamer' building castles on different planets.

- Challenges are there for us to embrace. Are you one of those that shy away from it?
- Time and planning are essential to your self-discovery. Are you aware of that?
- Don't become one of those that, after all their endeavours, lose their identities to the 'ruins of success'. * 'Ruins of success' depicts those men that allow their ego to rule them because they think they have achieved so much. What do you believe in?

CHAPTER TWELVE

Moment of Reflection

Everyone goes through a reflective moment at some point in his or her life, but the question is, how many of us learn from it? On the 20th of January 2007 at 12.17 pm, my wife gave birth to our princess. It was the most amazing experience I have ever had in my life. The cries and the screams all had a say in that special moment. There I sat with all the thoughts in my mind: I am now a Dad and her existence depends on 'me' for guidance and protection. She looked like me, I thought, and her essence was a reflection of me. I also thought that if I did not change my views towards life it would have a negative effect on her, and that if I failed to instil the ideals of the society in her, then life would not be worth living. There I stood, with all the things going on around me; I was probably in a trance. Many questions crowded my thoughts. I started to ponder on them, and I realized that her birth was a special moment, which, if I failed to change my views towards life, it might never be the same again. My reflective moment was there with me on the bed with her essence of joy.

The lesson is, if you go through life and neglect your special moments, then be prepared to face an untimely crisis of self-belief. Be careful with special moments, because they come with so many positivty which we have to learn from, if you neglect them, they will pass you by. Millions of us have black clouds over our heads and still dwell on them. Start now to conquer them one after the other. By accepting you have a problem, you are sincerely beginning the process of effecting changes. Set out a quiet time in your house and reflect upon problems, activities and life in general.

The three steps towards positive thinking depict ways we can necessarily effect a change through moments of reflection. It goes through identifying your circumstances, analysing them and from the outcome learning from them. Some people go through problems and circumstances but they never learn from them. The best option is to have a reflective moment; stop piling your problems up like heavy stones and getting caught by them. The term multiplicity of baggage's effect describes how people carry phases of problems and then get caught by this. Reflective moments are special moments and they are there to help us become better people.

As I sat one day, wondering about life in the midst of all its elements, I figured out my source of existence. If I tried to embrace it, it became an illusion and if I tried to avoid it, it became a 'headache'. How then could I amidst all these thoughts attain a sane attitude towards life? My life was hell, my work was dull, and my existence seemed to have been sown on rocky ground. Did I have the quality of a man who can effect a change in life? Couldn't I be myself? These are questions that plagued my mind as I realized the moment of truth. As I lay, it all seemed dull, dark and lonely, but one voice amidst it all assured me that everything would be fine. It was just a matter of time and, if I kept an honest face and worked towards my life, I would be a better person. Knock, knock came the sound of a postman who did not seem to understand that, at that point in time, I needed a quiet moment. To me it was an escape route to face reality, but when I weighed up my thoughts, I found out that that was the moment I realized that my life was going to change for the better. That was when I realized that the moment of truth has arrived. I then decided to write this poem:

Now I see what I see,
The perplexed sky I adore.
Now I see what I see,
Like the drooping dumpling; that sound.
Oh! That I may be encouraged,
A thousand times I wondered.
But life at my age could be fun
Even when the sun shines no more.

Maybe I should laugh,
But that surely will not help.
But maybe I should cry,
Even then, who might be of help?
For all the wrong reasons, I wailed
And searched and searched for a million answers
And there it stood
Like the prophet that soars.

Maybe it matters, maybe it doesn't.
But as far as I live, I will strive to succeed.
Even when my enemies applaud
I will embrace them.
For now is my moment,
A moment I will foretell.
Even in the midst of all things,
I will have my story to tell.

As you will have assembled a lot of messages through these few lines of mine, it reminds us about the millions of thoughts that pass through our minds every second. Use these moments to reflect upon your life and effect a change as I have already mentioned. 'I live my life the way I want it', that is true but remember, man has a purpose and if the purpose in life is not fulfilled, then we become worthless.

Reflective moments are there for us to use. There are so many ways and methods we can reflect upon our lives: yoga, meditation, the Hindu way of reflection, the Koran teaching and the biblical interpretations. All these can help instil confidence and reassurance that you are doing the right thing.

The Hide and Seek Rule

No, matter what phase we are in life, we do encounter problems and crisis situations at times. It is of prime importance to know how you deal with your circumstances. Some people apply certain principles, whiles others constantly deny the fact that they have problems. Self-deception has become increasingly common amongst many individuals in the society. Because of this, I have proposed the 'hide and seek' rule. It is a game played by kids and the point of the game is, you hide away in a dark corner in such a way that the person who is seeking you cannot find you. It is a game of seeking and finding, and the more you seek in places the greater the chances of finding the other person. In the end, the one that finds the opponent in dark corner wins, and vice versa.

Thus, this game basically applies to us humans. If you seek positive answers, you will definitely find them. Hiding away from your normal environment would certainly lead to positive answers. You can't seek answers in a hostile environment. We do have this knock-on effect when it comes to problems that had been unattended to in the past; but remember that your unconscious seems to dig into the past and then presents them in the conscious world. If our mind is in the continuum between our conscious and unconscious realms, then it seems quite obvious why the past plagues our mind from time to time. Have you ever had an accident or an event that took place that seems to present itself again from time to time, especially when similar situations occur? That basically explains how our human minds operate sometimes. The hide and seek rules coincides with reflective movement and constantly challenges your mind in all situations and circumstances. A few questions will help establish your status.

(1) How do you intend to prepare your mind for positive thinking?
(2) Why am I sometimes happy and sometimes sad?
(3) When you have problems, how do you approach them?
First, look at the problems, then raise all the possibilities and then start eliminating them one by one.
(4) When confused about certain subjects, how do you cope with them?
(5) Remember, for everything that happens to you, there is a reason; you either learn from it or you don't.

What are you filling you mind with?

(1) Books
(2) TV/programmes
(3) Friends and colleagues
(4) Exercise
(5) Work
(6) Positive clouds of energy

Seek out answers through meditation and you will definitely define the path you want to follow; the list is not exhaustive. In effect, all I am saying is, who are you?

Try and write something down in simple terms about your circumstances.

'Thinking the unthinkable' is not the way forward, rather a misconception to positive lessons.

The path to positive lessons is all around us and tends to shape our behaviours to conform to the 'ideals' of the society. These lessons are real and depict circumstances around us, which we sometimes neglect due to the 'modern way' of living. They come in the form of experience and the more we embrace them, the more life lessons we adopt. Have you ever watched one of the programmes on TV about when things go wrong? It depicts real life situations and events. It is quite comical when watching, but when you actually analyse the events as they happen, you will be surprised by the amount of 'teachings' you can obtain from it.

A child that learns to speak positively learns it from their parents, peers and society, and the opposite is also true.

Our Little Angels

We have used a lot of terms to define man, as he exists on earth. But do we really understand man in his full capacity? I believe as we plough through life with the deepest sincerity at heart, some of the reasoning behind man's existence can be explored. But the problem with us is that we constantly undermine nature's ways and I honestly believe it could be the reason why we don't seem to understand some of nature's ways. These mysteries have been put in place for a reason and if we try as humans to understand certain concepts of life, we could unravel the beauty of nature. Our gifts are bound in our essence and, for us to tap these free gifts of nature; we have to listen to ourselves. And for us to enjoy this journey, I believe that we have to listen to our little angels (consciences). They talk to us every day, but the problem we have is that we have moved away from our source of existence so much to the point where we basically glide like free birds. If we could understand the basic fact that there is a reason why we are here, then we would be glad to open our eyes to our guide. Our guide is our conscience and the earlier we begin to understand the secrets behind our existence the better. I have had so many experiences with my little angel, but most of those times I have failed to acknowledge it, only to realise that I had made the wrong decision. For you to grow in this concept of truth, you need to listen to your source of existence and banish the lackadaisical attitude of life.

The problem at times is the lack of self-belief, which we seem to exhibit as we embark on this long journey. We are not just talking about the physical existence but rather a compassionate phenomenon that leaves you wanting more. Every day of our lives, we hear the soft voice advising us on what to do. Sometimes we listen to it, other times we don't. I once thought about the elements of our conscience and added to that, I felt this strong sense that there must be something more to this existence. How come these strings of words do signify my essence? I couldn't find an answer to that and even if I could, I thought, it all seemed it was an impossible puzzle. But, on one occasion, this voice said it doesn't matter what you do, what class or religion you find yourself in, you are what you are. Our little angels work with us, sleep with us and do all kinds of things with us, but the sad truth is that most of us do not recognize that they are there to guide us. Most of us when confronted with these facts may resent it, but when we approach drastic situations, we then realize it is not a myth but rather a truth. The simple fact of life is that only those who seek it will surely find it. Understanding our conscience, and the way is works, is still a myth to the common man. Always set out on a quiet place to listen to your guide. The hardest parts to this are thinking about nothing and then waiting for answers. If you align yourself with nothing, then the rest is yours. The more you are willing to explore this avenue, the more you become acquainted with it. It is not by intelligence that you can listen to your source of existence but by the origin of our existence – 'God'. Most of the times I ask questions like, why do you use the word 'God' when you don't really believe in it? The answer they normally bring to the table is that they don't really believe in anything. This is not the subject I am going to explore for now, but if we sincerely believe that we do have our little angels then our world could be a lot better. What is self-discovery without an enviable attribute? I will leave you to figure that out.

Positive Lessons 12

- Reflective moments are there for us to use in effecting a positive change in our lives.
- Our reflection through birth basically aligns us with our essence.
- Become a being through which moral lessons are exhumed.
- Practical failures are failures that have gone beyond human questioning.
- If you can always justify your actions through good work and prayers, then you are really a man.
- Life can be a bitter experience if you do not abide by the core values of our existence.
- A silent minute could be the secret door to unravelling our essence. Try this at least once a day.
- Our mind is in a state of continuum between the conscious and subconscious. In between these could be that 'special moment'.
- Do not let your special moment pass without learning from it.
- Our hectic lifestyles have actually consumed our essences. Be careful of the things you do.
- Creativity is an art; the mind, a creator.
- The reasoning behind our essence is a myth to the common man.
- Every moment has its pictures locked in our minds; dreams that could be our wish fulfilment.
- The missing chapter in someone's life could be anything– wish fulfilment, a common problem.

CHAPTER THIRTEEN

Centre of Focus

Centering on our focus keeps us on the right path. The point of centering on your focal area is to ensure you keep to your plan. It is something you need to address each day of your life so that it becomes part of you. Each one of us slides along the elements of our focal energy. If we instil all our energy into achieving our goals, it becomes the better part of you. The most outstanding result is the explosive energy that sometimes arises due to immense concentration, which usually gives rise to success. The point is, concentrate on a problem and you will find so many ways to handle the problem. As an example, one of the tyres on my car once flew off on my way to work. The moment it happened, thousands of thoughts came to my mind. I first thought about the lesson I had had in fixing flat tyres. Secondly, I remembered the day a similar event happened when I was driving in my brother's company, and how he had fixed it by himself. Thirdly, I said to myself, 'I should have learnt how to do this, but instead I dissipated all the energy in something else.' I further thought of calling the car emergency services to fix the tyre for me. At last, the only alternative left was to do it myself. I eventually struggled and finally fixed it on my own. From then on, I learnt to do it through the centre of focus. I concentrated and focused all my energy on it, which resulted in a positive achievement. This simply means that if we channel our energy towards self-discipline then we will be like the 'reservoir of self-discipline'. On the other hand, if one's energy is chanelled towards negative ideas, such ideas will constitute your downward slope away from self- attainment.

Have you reached the centre of your focus? If you have, what lessons have you learnt? Try these simple basic steps:

- What is your goal?
- How do I attend to my goal?
- Seek positive advice.
- Adopt positive attitudes to life,
- Align all your energy towards achieving your dreams.
- Remember that some have high focal energy while others don't
- Find the best way to sort your problems

A typical example of our centre of focus is our everyday job. Many of us concentrate on the wage system since it is our source of sustenance. It is not by choice but by our way of living. If you disregard the theme of our modern ways then you are heading towards a total disaster. Imagine a month without an income in our modern society that would be like pining your hope on something that doesn't exist. How then do we focus on a daily basis when we are stripped off our wages? It is simple: if you want to carry on with life, then you have to focus on the things that matter. What I have observed is that for us to focus on any task, energy needs to be expended and the price we pay for this expended energy is the pay cheque we get at the end of the day. Now what the centre of focus does is to ensure you revolve around your focal energy in order to achieve your goal. The reason why we centre on our focal centres is that, for us to become great achievers, we have to make sure we stay on course, and I believe this is one of the downfalls of many of us. Because of so many distractions in our modern society, it is easy to stray from your destined path. Since we have different centres, it is of prime importance that we know our pursuits in life. Those who understand this concept are winners. On the other hand, the ones who stray from this centre and never return are the ones that have been consumed by modern pressures. I do not have to perform any miracles for you to know that our essence, which incorporates our willpower, maintains us in the right track. How then do we achieve this? If you look back to chapter 2, on positive thoughts, you will find a lot there on how you can stay on course. I have this slogan, which I normally use: 'if I don't conquer, that is my loss and if I do conquer, I get really scared of losing'. This basically drives my will to succeed and empowers me with an ever-fulfilling need to succeed. I have noticed from my experiences that our circumstances and experiences in life tend to mould our character for the better or for the worse. It basically depends on the individuals who find themselves in such a situation to act according to their train of thoughts.

Positive Lessons 13

- Planning is an essential part of humans' lives. Do the obvious things first.
- Address your problems each day and you will be pleased with how your mind works.
- If we align ourselves with our focal energy, our thwarted realizations would be a thing of the past.
- What is your centre of focus? Are you aware of your basic needs?
- People just don't know how to focus, and that's why failure becomes a major part of them.
- Our goals are what we work towards; the rest is our motives.
- Our characters define us as a person; our goals test our strength.

- When it comes to attending to needs, man becomes a wizard at it.
- If we create a path without a proper reasoning to it, it could be the beginning of a dicey adventure.
- When a man focuses on a task, his mental energy could be related to energy in Calories. This basically tells you about the amount of energy expended as we embark on a task.
- Our centre of focus drives our will to succeed and empowers us with an ever-fulfilling need to succeed.
- My life is what I owe, but my centre is personal.

CHAPTER FOURTEEN

Journey of Life

Life is not worth living if its purpose is not fulfilling among all other elements. Our purpose circles around life and when we analyse it, you will find that life is not meaningful without a purpose attached to it. Our journey towards fulfilling our purpose is quite a difficult adventure. This is because when faced with various choices we seem to get confused in making the right choice. Our choice depends on our psyche, environment and probably our culture. Culture and reflective moments play a significant role towards fulfilling our destiny in the 21st century. Destiny is fate, and chooses from among many other things, the heart that desires to achieve. There are mixed conceptions about our views on destiny. My advice is, be wise, for a wise man seeks answers, and reasons, then acts upon them. Our journey in life is a journey towards self-realization. If you sail on the right course, then your fulfilment of life will be accomplished; if not, it will be a wasted journey. Life is a state of struggle, even if amongst the contours of our struggle there comes a ray of hope. Whatever you want to achieve on this planet comes with a drop of sweat. Life has designed this stage for those who are ready to fight towards self-realization and release themselves from the shackles of self-pity and condemnation. While for those who have already lost the battle, the question is, what stuff are you made of? There are three phases towards self-actualization:

(i) Those who strive to achieve, but fail to realize the elements of life, and get consumed by those elements.
(ii) Those who strive wisely and still recognize that life has its consequences.
(iii) Those who fail because they didn't attempt it at all.

From these, we all have lessons to learn from life because life is full of mysteries and circumstances.

The journey of life starts from birth and then aligns itself with the contours of our existence. Our essence towards existence cannot be questioned because, even amongst other animals on the planet, man stands out against all organisms and elements. We are classed as superior and even when we choose to deny it, everything around us seems to be pointing in the same direction. Many questions have been asked about our existence and why we are here, the most definite answer is, I have been created for a purpose and that purpose could be related to many things. Many of us don't seem to question our minds and we seem to get caught up by circumstances. We seem to plough the same furrows of life and grab whatever crosses our path. Some of us seek happiness, wealth, career, success, love, luck and much more. But all this throws various challenges across our path. The search for what we want depends on several factors; but one of the factors that reinforces it is our self-belief. We search for wealth, happiness, love, etc, but do we find them? If there is any justification for our purpose, how do we search for answers? And if we do find them, what's next? From our view of life, man is constantly in the sphere of wants, but fails to realize that enough is enough. Some embrace these 'notions' even to death, and get mixed up in their self-purpose. To be self-satisfied is one of the qualities people seem not to have; we have lost these qualities in the battle of 'I want it now' and, as a result, get enslaved by it. The reasons for this are simple, and there are many examples I have given earlier on how wealth has ruined the lives of so many people. Remember, be wise about it, and you will succeed. The journey of life starts with a step and, as you continue on the journey, there are a few obstacles that may confront you.

- Issues of marriage
- Issues of love
- The fight for who we are
- Careers and ambitions
- What if I fail?
- Can I really achieve?
- What is my destiny?
- Friends
- Others

Always remember, life is not a bed of roses. For those who believe they can change the course of destiny, success is definitely theirs in the end. The issue of marriage can be viewed as the union of two people by divine observance. Your purpose could be to have a happy family and drive them in the 'ideals' of society. Modern-day marriages are looked upon as a driveway through life that may or may not end well. It is up to you how you look at marriage, but always remember that certain marriages are not mean to be. Therefore, if you discover the road to happiness through marriage, keep up the good work and fight the evils that plague it.

I remember the story of Romeo and Juliet. Love heals all things and by that, if you love, and love is you, then the possibilities towards a successful journey in life will be fulfilled. If we were to decide to place a tag on every person on this planet, we would realize that many of us are floaters in our society; we just don't know where and how to fit in. The answer for you is to wake up and start living. Have another look at chapter 12, on reflective moments, because that will help you understand the reasons why we are here. We fight for careers, ambitions, etc, but we forget that if a farmer goes to the farm without his farm tools, he has failed in establishing his identity there. This is simple. A lot of us struggle without any reason, because we fail to do the things we ought to do first; therefore try to do first things first. If you have an ambition to become a pharmacist, for example, you have to take the necessary steps to find out if this career is for you. You should visit a careers adviser, read up on a pharmacy degree and so on. The point is, people aim high in life, but fail to organize themselves carefully. The normal question people always ask is, 'What if I fail?' Failure is a good lesson, which we all go through at some point in our lives. Don't get confused by its consequences. Whatever you believe in your mind can be achievable. Learn from obvious facts; friends could be your strength or weakness. If you work in the path of darkness and still believe that there may a ray of light, then you must be joking. The reasoning behind this is simple, imagine yourself in the midst of friends who discourage the good works of others, it is only a matter of time and you will begin to operate on the same frequency as they do. Associate yourself with people with the same principles, but if you mingle with friends with negative attributes, then you have to decide where you want to be. There are known facts that we all learn unconsciously and manifest the unconscious thought we prefer. But remember, the unconscious also manifests itself on certain occasions; it could be when you have made up your mind to sort out your life-purpose. Life is a journey with various consequences; embrace it, listen to your heart, seek the right answers and think about the path that you want to follow. As I have said earlier, beware of negative influences and become 'you'. Don't allow things that do not make sense to influence your destiny. Align yourself with your life and enjoy the fruits of life.

Positive Lessons 14

- Life has a purpose and when it is not fulfilled it becomes a wasted journey.
- A wise man is one who seeks answers and reasons and then acts upon them.
- Destiny is fate and it chooses from the many, the heart that desires to achieve.
- The 'seek and find' concept is one that many of us acknowledge, but when it comes down to practical terms, it then becomes a problem. *My advice is to understand the things around you and start living.
- The 'I want' concept seems to have enslaved man right to his grave. 'Enough is enough, should be our anthem.
- The journey of life starts off with a step, so be sure you start off on the right foot or you will definitely be cycling on a windy road!
- Marriage is looked upon nowadays as a driveway through life that may or may not end well. To me that's just the beginning of another challenge in life. *My advice is, be very careful about the messages of love, because 'love' has been convicted to its very end.
- Friends are the greatest assets to your progress; associate with the wrong ones and that will be your downfall.
- Make an effort to ensure that you are organized because this will ultimately boost your self-esteem.

CHAPTER FIFTEEN

Leaders of Tomorrow

Many of us find ourselves managing businesses, homes, schools, etc, but are we true leaders of today who can inspire leaders of tomorrow? Leaders of tomorrow can be seen as you and I, who are constantly bombarded by the ideals of society. If we have confidence in ourselves, then that would be a step closer towards preparing for our responsibilities. The former US President Clinton did not become one of the most influential people overnight; he worked towards it through clear positive steps of self-attainment. The former British Prime Minister, Blair, was one of the most prominent and eloquent leaders of recent times who used his communicational skills to charm the whole world. Even though these two leaders were different individuals, they both had the characteristics of true leaders. But we also have leaders all over the world who do not reflect the qualities of a true leader. The problem is that some of us take these qualities as 'ideals', without truly understanding the meaning behind them. Some true leaders are born, but others achieve it through acquired learning. Have you got what it takes to be a true leader on this planet? If you believe in yourself and believe in the principles of true leadership then this path is definitely for you.

When I left home to start secondary school, I was quite young, like the other students who had just gained entry at the same time. It was a mixed feeling of anxiety and freedom, but that was just the start of an intriguing journey. It was very frightening, because we were nervous when faced with challenges. At that stage I unconsciously established the fact that I could be a true leader. I was made both the class prefect and the house captain at the same time due to my excellent qualities. It was a big challenge for me but I went through it with a clear positive attitude. My life changed from an individual who was naturally shy to someone who voiced his opinion and influenced a great number of students. A true leader should have the following qualities:

- Tactfulness
- Assertiveness
- Team spirit
- Self-discipline
- Integrity
- Vision seeking
- Observance
- Power of Persuasion
- Motivational skill

A true leader should have the enviable qualities that always make him stand out among others. Being tactful means being discreet and diplomatic. Being assertive demands that a leader stand on his words, but doing so requires diplomacy. People will understand what messages you are trying to relay depending on how you play your cards. As a true leader, you must move with the crowd, for it is said that 'no man is an island'. Team spirit is not just about working together, but encouraging each other towards the attainment of a goal. My ideology of team spirit is the reason behind why the whole world has not collapsed. The simple reason is not rocket science, but demands that the unified structure of a government is made up of several units, which represents government affairs. If one of the units collapses, the government will start to foresee problems, so each unit has actually contributed to the building of a solid governmental system. And it is possible for the government to stand, due to this unified effort. There is a message here for those who think that they cannot work in harmony with some people. Be warned, because no system can work on its own; you have to start to learn to accommodate and work closely with people, as they can be the key towards success in your career or life. If I were to vote which quality was most relevant, I would choose self-discipline, because not only does it establish your identity, but also it portrays every facet of you. What people see in you will make them believe in your concepts or dismiss them.

A leader who has no self-control and does not know where to stop in any situation might be endangering his position. As it is said, 'Wisdom consists in knowing where to stop in everything one does.' Self-discipline goes with integrity, knowing your facts and ideals. Most leaders at times forget that people depend on them for so many things and that any step towards self-destruction would definitely send out conflicting messages. It could be in the form of a misjudgement, because they feel they are seen as leaders and therefore, as a matter of fact, nothing that comes from them could be seen as wrong. In effect, a leader could mislead thousands of souls, and eventually lead them to self-damnation, so as a leader, you have to be wise in your dealings with people, for a lot of eyes are on you. Integrity and self-discipline are inseparable; your status is your power. To be someone amongst many who influences the decisions of others, you must possess certain qualities, such as loyalty, honesty, truthfulness and self-discipline. These boost your ego and single you out among the many as ' a man of special characteristics'. The integrity of man is second nature to him, but if he loses it, it could be lost forever. Many search, and many see goals that are clear to them, but do they achieve them? No they don't. The problem a lot of us have is that we generally have a vision for success, but we deny ourselves the path towards achieving it. Most of us have visions in life that we aspire to, but how do we go about realizing them? Our attitude towards our vision undermines our achievements; because we are not focusing on achieving it, we fail or fall by the wayside. Due to our lackadaisical attitude towards life, we blame everything for our downfall, only to realize later it was our failure. Jumping from one vision to another is another reason why you may not have achieved your goal. Many of us seek, but do we find? I always ask myself this question, but to my amazement, it wasn't clear to me what my vision was, and then it came to me. If I can influence millions of souls out there of the virtues of life, then I will have contributed towards instilling good qualities in their lives.

As we progress through the 21st century, true leadership has begun to be recognized. The reason for this stems from the ever-changing nature of society; as different religions and cultures clash in different settings, 'things are bound to be said'. Therefore, leaders of tomorrow should be on their guard against elements that are cropping up in society at a very alarming rate. Don't let 'hearsay' be part of your decision-making process, or you could end up giving mistaken judgement based on false rumours. We have all made decisions concerning our lives, but the decision you make today, if you keep to it, will lead you through the rest of your life. Don't let poor decision making form the major part of you, and avoid making too many decisions that are conflicting. True leaders make decisions and stand by them, which is why they would die for them. Most decision- making process go through steps of reasoning and acceptance. If you make a decision, there are simple basic steps you have to follow to ensure you have made the right one. Look at the following examples:

- Maybe this could be the only way out .
- If I take this route, there will be less harm done.
- This route definitely makes more sense.

These are some of the many steps we take to come to a decision, but above all, have we made the right decision?

There is no right or wrong decision, but it is the path that it leads to that makes it a wrong or a right one.

Power of persuasion is another good quality a true leader must possess. True leaders of tomorrow should be able to win the hearts and minds of the many in conflict situations. A true leader should know what he wants and go for it using his persuasive powers. Making decisions on conflicting issues could go either way. It could lead to civil wars or holy wars, etc. so persuasive powers tell you who is a leader and confirms his integrity in the minds of his people. Are you a true leader? You can try this at work, at school, at home, but don't use it for the wrong reasons, because it could hunt you. The power of persuasion can only work if people believe in you as a true leader whose rare gift is shown to them. Try as much as possible to utilize your special gift in any situation or circumstance you find yourself in. Decision- making tells people a lot about you. Becoming a true leader is not an easy journey; you will come across decision-making processes that are strange or difficult to you, but that may be the only way out, so be prepared to deal with them.

My idea of a motivator is seen as someone whose presence instils confidence in people: they trust you; acknowledge your weaknesses, yet you nevertheless instil a positive attitude in them. Such are the qualities of a true leader. To motivate people, you must be aware of obstacles coming your way, but using all you have learnt in these previous chapters, you should be able to motivate others, in other to produce positive outcomes.

A leader with vision understands where he wants to be, so he decides on what to do, sets targets and sets off on this journey. He is a master in his games and always reassures everyone that he is on the right path. He does understand the uncertainties of life, but he prepares for them. He takes risks, but guards against shortcomings; a true leader understands all this in addition to understanding the laws of the land. If you are in the course of becoming a true leader whose good work will stand the test of time, my question is, are you ready?

Positive Lessons 15

- You and I are leaders of tomorrow; therefore if you start making preparations now, you will definitely reward your endless effort at some point.
- Even though different leaders might come from different races, background, cultures and religions, the true qualities of a leader always reflects in their characteristics. Seek out these qualities in different leaders.
- Challenges are there for us to embrace as we embark on this journey. Be ready, because it is going to be a tale of never ending lessons.
- If you find yourself engaged in disseminating information to a group of people, be careful how you relay messages to them; speak in a very sensible way, using an understanding approach. Your mannerism at any point of contact reflects who you are.
- We talk about 'team spirit', but from my understanding, in simplistic terms, if you cannot deal with your fellow humans, whom else can you actually deal with? Perhaps one of the species in the animal kingdom, I guess?

- Understanding man and his dignity is underpinned in self-discipline. Become a leader whose presence is the talk of the nation.
- Remember, we all are leaders, probably at school, home, work and so on. But be careful how you throw around words because certain comments could kill a man's will to live.
- Are you who you say you are? Just because you found yourself in an enviable position does not make it right to step on every toe that happens to be in your way.
- Too many conflicting decisions can be deeply damaging. *Be on your guard. True leaders make decisions and stand by them. Are you one of them?
- The power to accept mistakes and then learn from them makes you an ever-cherishable leader. Do not decry this but rather acknowledge it as one of the lessons we ought to acquire during our lives.
- To bring out the best in a man is one of the most amazing gifts we all should try to acknowledge. True leaders know how to go about these things.
- A true leader knows the vision of the people. Therefore, through those qualities, which are bestowed in them, they can see those whose heart is edging towards their dreams. How they accomplish the vision of the people through their intuitive character is what amazes their followers. The uncertainty of life is what amazes us, but a true leader understands that and reinforces his positivity amongst men who desire it.

CHAPTER SIXTEEN

A Positive Reward; Sacrifice

Sacrifice involves forfeiting something valuable to achieve something of still higher value. Men strive to achieve, but sometimes fail to realize the importance of sacrifice in life. Sacrifice is a positive action that displays elements of sincerity amongst individuals fighting for a just cause. Sacrifice comes with reward, and that is one of the most satisfying ventures you can ever get into. Sacrifices are made, but are they always made for the right reasons? Most achievements on the planet come as results of sacrifices. Man constantly underestimates the value of sacrifices. However, if we see things the way wise men do, then we shall start learning how to make sacrifices. For example, I became a graduate at the school of pharmacy in Portsmouth because of the sacrifice I had made towards my academic career. It was a sacrifice based on years of active learning, which resulted in the acquired knowledge and skills needed to become an accredited pharmacist. For you to succeed in life, you have to start making sacrifices. Realization of one's dream starts with a step in the right direction, but if sacrifice misses your path, then what is left is only an idea. My reasons for saying this stems from years of active sacrifices towards building a career. So, if you want to start any successful journey, then start mapping out plans towards the sacrifice involved. Since we all pay a price to achieve something, and that is through sacrifice, we all have to forgo something to get something else. If you are not willing to pay a price, then start thinking now. Many of us live in this realm of 'I want it now', but fail to understand that concept of 'if you get something out of nothing the value becomes worthless'. Therefore, plan precisely what you want to do, take into account the time needed to achieve it, embrace sacrifice and then begin your journey.

Sacrifice can occur at any level of achievement. To get rewarded for being a good office employee, you have to pay the price of staying at work and working long hours to get the extra money. If you want to become a successful actress, then you have to start learning how to memorize your lines and to act upon them. But, all in all, it requires years of sacrifice. Sacrifice is the price you have to pay to get anything. Most of us believe in the price of achievement and that is why we do what we do. If, for example, my Mum decided not to sacrifice the nine months of active gestational period, it would not have been possible for me to write these few lines. In effect, we have seen the value of sacrifice. It is a priceless gift, laid out for humans to use to achieve their dreams. Realization of one's dream basically rests on sacrifice as a base and then projects everything that comes along. We all talk about sacrifices made to achieve a great deal, but have we actually talked about what it takes to make these sacrifices? If you think about the sacrifices we make on this earth knowingly and unknowingly, it could amass to a million fortunes. The point is, sacrifice comes with a price, but if we owe it to ourselves to make a perfect sacrifice, then these rewards should not be our goal. Our goal should be that of learning to make a perfect sacrifice.

My ideology about sacrifice is that of the things we do in life and my search for a perfect sacrifice seems to be intriguing. For all I know, any sacrifice comes with a reward, but if as humans we can learn not to concentrate on the rewards, we will go far in the future. I have talked about our boundaries in life in Chapter 5, but remember, sacrifice is one of the virtues, which can release countless blessings to our everyday struggle. As I have stated, even though man's understanding has been bridged to a certain point, there are certain signs that can help you cross the road to success. I believe that sacrifice could carry those signs. It is not a matter of science or religion, but if you believe in natural laws, then you will understand where I am coming from. If you haven't learnt anything from this chapter, please do consider sacrifice, because I believe that it can free you from the shackles of this society and equip you with an ever-cherishable appeal. Most of us go around mentioning good qualities in others. At times we get confused over how men in this modern world can still be of value to society. If you ask me, I will tell you that sacrifice can help you achieve a lot, if you let it. Work on it on a daily basis. You don't have to get paid for everything you do on this planet. Always remember that for you to have reached where you are at this moment, a lot of people had to make sacrifices at some point for you. No matter how little it might appear, sacrifice could go a long way in instilling those qualities that you seem to have neglected. Don't for any reason despise the sacrifice of others, but rather embrace them, because sacrifice in itself is an epitaph of moral blessings in disguise. Live with these lessons and you will present yourself as a satisfied person with good reasons at the root of your life. It's not by outrageous mistake that we have set foot on the planet, but by carefully planned phenomena which you and I seem to search for as we march along the windy road of life. People who believe in sacrifice understand its concept and that is why I believe it is one of the greatest virtues in life. Embrace sacrifice and realize your own blessings. You are blessed, so keep up the good work. Remember, it is only those who seek a better understanding of life that will embrace life's lessons, so please advise yourself on the best tactics for this approach.

- Now, are you willing to make sacrifices that could either make or break you?
- The road to sacrifice is a long one. Are you willing to take it?
- If you are ready to embark on realization of one's self, be prepared to embrace sacrifice as a tool of progress.

The moment you decide to make a big sacrifice towards self-attainment, that moment is the start of your success. Don't miss your moment of countless blessings.

Positive Lessons 16

- Men have failed to realize the importance of sacrifice.
- Sacrifice can be seen as a positive outlook that portrays an element of sincerity amongst individuals willing to fight for the just cause.
- Sacrifice normally comes with a reward at the end of it.
- Sacrifice basically tests our character, and that alone could strengthen our character.
- In sacrifice lies one of the virtues of life.
- Realization of one's dream starts off with a step in the right direction, but if sacrifice misses your path, what's left is only an idea.
- No achievement can effectively take place without sacrifice being involved.
- Sacrifice is the price you need to pay to achieve anything useful. The problem is that most of us do not want to pay that price.
- The concept of ' I want it now' should be erased from our minds; it's one of the reasons why men have gone against their will.
- If you get something out of nothing, it is of no value.
- Plan ahead in terms of what you want to achieve, but take into account the time needed to achieve it. Remember, time is of value to those who value it.
- The moment you decide to embark on the road to self-attainment through sacrifice, that moment is your moment of truth.

CHAPTER SEVENTEEN

Old habits die hard

We all have habits that we exhibit in our everyday lives. Such patterns of behaviour have been acquired through the active learning phase. Man uses his habits as templates that drive him towards making new decisions and dealing with circumstances. For instance, when it comes to the issue of smoking, most of us who smoke have the habit of smoking first thing in the morning; this is a habit we can change for the better. Remember, you cannot erase old habits from your memory, but rather you can create new paths towards self-recovery. Our minds are constantly bombarded by the stresses of modern living and for us to cope we need to have habits, which helps us to decrease our mental usage, in order to cope with these circumstances. Our minds work on a reservoir of information and refer to it whenever a familiar situation recurs. Thus, habits make our lives easier; they are pathways that make our day-to-day activities worth accounting for. Our habits could be our fears or our strengths, depending on what they are. Aristotle stated that we are what we repeatedly do. Excellence then, is not an act but a habit. From this, we can infer that if we align ourselves with positive attitudes, then this becomes part of us. If what we do every day is part of us, we are constantly expressing our habits. In order to deal with our environment, there are three steps towards positive thinking that ensure that we address our situations and make them better. If we instil these steps into our daily routine, it will then become part of us; therefore our habits determine our ways of expression, which are familiar to us. If these three steps become a habit, then realization of one's dream becomes a pronounced statement of intent. My advice is that you make these steps your habit and improve your life. Remember that a single habit may possibly lead to destruction of one's reputation. For example, if I normally act on my negative thoughts, such as addressing an issue in an abusive and unhealthy manner, then, as far as that is concerned, my self-esteem will be questionable. In this case, my habit of addressing an issue had become a bad habit.

Good habits show others our ways and this strikes people when they approach you. From my understanding, good habits these days seem to have been displaced and bad habits seem to be rearing their ugly head in our society. I remember when I was a child and how my Dad taught me how to greet people first thing in the morning. It was a habit I grew up with and to date I still greet people with 'Good morning' when I have opportunity to do so. The problem I have noticed is that many of us despise the morning greetings and ask questions like, 'What is good about the morning'? To me, it is amazing how modern society is shifting its values. The first time I heard that question I was shocked because I felt that it displayed total negativity. Good habits are there for us to emulate. Let us not shy away from the obvious and believe we are doing the right thing. My opinion about bad habit is that, it is a matter of what you have learnt. But, if we are people of distinctive character, I believe we ought to do the right thing. One example of bad habit, which keeps recurring, is that some people open their bowels and release a foul smell only to turn around and laugh. To this day, many people don't see this as a bad habit but rather treat it as some kind of joke.

The point is, are we a generation that is heading towards a total disaster or are we just a mere representation of our race? The problem is that most of us ignore it, but I will tell you it's an obvious fact that things we take for granted tend to haunt us at a later stage. What do we tell our youth who witness such 'indecencies'? The point I am trying to put across is that these bad habits seem to be the order of the day; so most of us actually think we are doing the right thing. Referring back to the salutations that we tend to neglect. In Africa, when you come across an elderly person and you don't acknowledge them, especially during the morning, you are considered to have 'thingified' the person. In other words, you have classed that person as an 'inanimate object', which is considered very disrespectful in that context. To me, if I were to start naming all the bad habits we exhibit, it would be like the story that was once told that never ended. If we try to stop all these habits and move on to the next step towards positive attainment, I believe we are doing the right thing. Most of us should start weaning ourselves off these habits and start embracing good habits, which in effect can lead to self-discovery. If you honestly believe in good habits, then this book is for you. Most of the time we know what to do, but because of the society we belong to it tends to become the source of our vices. If you understand that good habits cannot be bought in the market, then you will listen to every anguished cry of those who have fallen because of the habits they can't let go. The problem at times with humans is that we do not understand ourselves and, even when we do, we try to do the opposite of what is right to see what might happen. But most of the time we dig a pit for ourselves, only to realize that we have created a lot of mess along the way. Only those who finally make it tell the stories of their vices. Most of them are still wallowing in their thoughts and disbelieving how they finally got to where they are. I would repeat this: those who understand the concept of willpower will know that you don't start something you can't finish. The best solution at times is not to attempt something you can't control. If you sincerely know in your heart that you are dealing with the impossible, leave it and move forward. Most of the time, because of the inquisitive nature of man, we consciously want to try anything and when we find ourselves struggling, we tend to blame it on something.

The good news is that good habits are there for us to emulate. But the bad ones are there to destroy everything we have built on. Our brain understands human nature, and it tends to display certain characteristics; that is why at times it amazes me. The point is, most of the time we can't understand how it works. For instance, there is this system I normally use to operate pharmacy systems at work. One day, I found myself in an unfamiliar environment and, because I hadn't used the system, I couldn't operate it. I was furious and disappointed with myself because I knew I had used that system some time ago. I then decided to start fiddling with the system and to my great surprise, it was as if a door just opened and everything I knew just emerged. The reason is simple, as I have discussed: our minds work as an information reservoir and look back to whenever similar situations occurred. Imagine how much energy we spend every day on active thinking. What our brain does is to reduce that energy by recalling these pathways and re-channelling them to other parts of the body that needs them. To me, that is an excellent piece of the 'machine' that we have.

The problem with the bad habits is that they always remain with us. So keep your bad habits to a minimum and fight them with everything you have. If you cultivate the habit of doing the right thing, then you will excel in your wishes. Man does understand these concepts, but why we stray from the right path still amazes me.

We are all accountable for our actions. If you want to become an influential person in society then start learning how to change from old habits to new ones. The power of positive thinking should help in this case. Always remember, old habits once in a while manifest themselves in certain circumstances, so be on your guard.

Positive Lessons 17

- Our habits depict our ways and this is what makes us who we are.
- Remember, you cannot erase your old habits but you can redesign new paths towards self-discovery.
- Habits make our life easier and define 'who' we are.
- If we walk in the positive realms of life then doing so becomes a part of us.
- Our habits determine our ways of expression, which are familiar to us.
- Our mental faculty has been designed for a purpose, habit forming a part of the process.
- ' I thought of something is a is a thought, but the habit of actually thinking could be the key to great thinkers.
- Good habits are there for us to keep, but the problem is our vices.
- The art of shouting all the time is a habit but the will to stop it expresses our character.

CHAPTER EIGHTEEN

An idle mind is the devil's playground

The practical human mind has ways of dealing with situations as I have mentioned earlier. It approaches different situations, circumstances and events with different outlooks. Firstly, it quickly embraces the negatives and slowly comes to terms with positives. Take for instance the development of children, as they go through the cycle of behavioural learning. This makes them who they are. At close observation, you will notice that they embrace bad behaviours at a glance. If we instil such negativity in these kids, it will eventually become their way of life as 'a child learns from what he or she lives'.

An idle mind basically entails a mind that has not been challenged in life. The challenges of life are many and they live with us. What this deceptive mind does is to block off everything and live in the zone of unreality. In effect, you begin to think of things outside of your existence, to reason without putting much thought into it. You view every situation as work and therefore shy away from the energy-dependent zone of discomfort.

The human mind is unlimited and with the deceptive mind at work, it is obvious why the idle mind steals time to play. People who embrace such a concept get themselves sucked into this sphere of retrogression. They find it very hard to cope with life because to them, life seems very complex. The problem they have is that they have lived with this kind of condition for years and therefore to break this cycle of habits seems very challenging. To make matters worse, most of them live with people, friends and family who are also confused by such thoughts. In effect, there is no way out because no one amongst them has got the fighting spirit to deal with such evil. I vividly remember an event that took place during my younger days. One of my friends was caught up in a fight between his parents and that was a reality check. He rushed round to my Daddy's house with his hands to his head. He screamed and shouted for help as he approached our compound. My Dad asked him what was the matter, and he replied with a trembling voice, ' My Dad wants to kill my Mum,' My Dad quickly rushed round to his house and was shocked at how he was received. My friend's Dad was unemployed and an alcoholic, who tackled his problems with the bottle and believed that his wife had contributed heavily to his downfall. His wife was a schoolteacher who inspired a lot of people around the neighbourhood and many envied her reputation. Their problems reached the point where physical abuse became the order of the day and this made their children intervene. But by then it was too late, as it was not long before their Mum died due to the ill effects of depression. From that very moment, the children left their Dad because they believed he embraced evil for good and had wasted the life of their Mum. All in all, he had become the victim of an idle mind, which plagues millions of souls out there. Don't become a victim of such evil. If you try to extrapolate the effect of an idle mind on society and the accompanying damage on social progress that would be classed as preposterous. The reason for this comes from the reduction in the workforce that contributes to the wealth of a nation. The problem with these people is that their minds are constantly in search of something out of reach, so they basically live life through self-pity and dejection.

Even if you're amongst the educated ones, if you decide to engage in these activities that do not keep your mind occupied then you will become a victim of the devil's playground. My question is, if you are not feeding your brain with positive thoughts, what are you feeding it with? Be careful how you go about executing certain thoughts because it could be for the wrong reasons. Think back to the march of 'drooping dumplings' that sap society's wealth without putting anything back into society. Most of them must circle around the contours of an idle mind. The danger is; if you dwell in such gloominess for long, it will become a big challenge to start seeing life from a different perspective. This is because to these victims, life is not worth living. They blame society for their mishaps and accuse everyone that crosses their path. They never see anything positive in life and then in the end; they give up and suffer from various ill-health conditions. I believe that each one of them needs to address the situation and start living again.

Some people pass through life without letting life pass through them. If you want to start enjoying the fruits of life, then you have to start challenging your mind. Don't let it wither away like the seed planted in a rocky soil. Any playground that is open to an external influence will definitely experience a lot of problems. Our idle mind is like the thief that creeps up on us from time to time. Whenever I sit down to analyse the situation, one thing keeps coming to my mind and that is, 'the wasted force of human existence'. The problem here is that most of the time, they seem to form this network of friends, which sluggishly depend on us for their existence. My search for such attitudes keep on plaguing my mind because I just can't understand the reasons why people embrace such situations and let it control their lives. If our minds are bottled up in our essence, how come we stray from our very existence and do as we please? I believe that a majority of people who dwell in these situations become enslaved by this and as a result become victim of such a sad existence. The key to understanding human nature lies in the heart of man. The only way out is if these people could understand what life is all about, and then I believe they would change for the better. I have searched for answers as to why we have been made the way we are, and most of the time it points towards the understanding of human nature. We have been created with so much knowledge that the things we can do sometimes are just beyond our comprehension. Why we laze about with no thought to life seems to be the impending problem. If man was given everything he needed without actually working for it, life would be very uninteresting and that is why people can only achieve their dreams if they consciously coincide with nature's elements. The problem we have is that our thoughts revolve around the spheres of evil. If you don't understand these ideologies in life, then when you are approached with so many vices it is left for you to reject them and carry on along your path towards self-discovery. The lessons here are that man's foolish thoughts at times could be his weakness if he allows them to be his strength. If we understand the concept, then the rest is ours. I have found myself in certain situations: some I have challenged, while some I have fallen for. But the good thing here is that, for everything that happens to us, if we do learn from it then we should be prepared to tell stories that will change people's lives positively.

Don't let your playground be your downfall. Fight the evil that plagues your mind and set forth towards this wonderful life's long lessons. For any level of self-attainment, an idle mind will definitely have a negative influence on it. Don't become a victim and subject yourself to a lot of unnecessary pressure in life. Don't become part of the reason why our society is heading towards its very end.

Seek your destiny and stop the thief that might creep in from time to time. We all pass through these 'mind states' from time to time, but it is the survivors that discuss them. Express yourself and become free from this bondage. Any concept that is worth idealizing must be of prime importance to man. Keep the spirit going.

Positive Lessons 18

- Our mind is bottled up in our essence; depending on how we use it will ultimately open doors to our understanding. 'Innocence is a blessing'.
- The key to understanding human nature lies in the hearts of men.
- A dubious character seems to be acquired easily while 'an enviable character' is a struggle.
- An idle mind seems to be a mind that shies away from challenges.
- With the disciplined mind at work, it is obvious why the idle mind steals time to play.
- Life seems very complex to those who get consumed by it.
- A nation's wealth lies in its workforce but the habit of becoming idle will be a curse on it.
- Why does man's thought easily revolve around the spheres of evil? Answer: man's thought is a source of his weakness.
- The challenges of life are intriguing to the reflective man; to the idle man, they represent a complex.
- The fruits of life will never get to the hands of those that dwell in an unchallenged atmosphere.
- Seek out your destiny and prevent the thieves that creep up in the night from time to time.
- We all go through these phases from time to time; only the winners talk about them.
- The lessons of life educate us and equip us with the weapons of life. To the mind that is weak, I say, wake up and start living.

CHAPTER NINETEEN

Are we sharing the same dream?

I would look at the question in two different ways. Firstly, people whom we respect and how they influence us. Secondly, friends and how they actually influence our dreams. Many of us find it difficult to express ourselves properly in the midst of our friends and as a result suppress our views. Such views could be the ' ultimate ideology 'to self-discovery, but due to our ways it then gets 'brushed under the carpet'. One instance is the classical example of an assumed conception about wealth. One of my colleagues at work came to me and made the statement that riches were everything and that if he were given £2 million it would sustain him and solve all his problems. I quickly disagreed, and said, 'Once you have that money, it will be the beginning of your worries. Because you wouldn't want to go back to the way you were, it would be a fight to ensure that your money really grows.' That's just the beginning, and from this you could see that if he really thought about his statement, he would not have come up with it. Even though we all look at life from different perspectives, the problem is not having a clearly defined goal that pushes us between the boundaries of our needs. I usually strive to ensure that at any point in time I know where I am going in life. But at times, uninviting friends could become a thorn in the flesh.

The constant bombardment coming from all sides of life could push you over the edge. They come in the form of a friend but have camouflaged themselves in order to own you or get as much information out of you as they can. They basically twist your mind and ensure that at any point in time they have a glimpse of your circumstances. All I am saying is, beware of wolves in sheep's clothing that have for years been in the close circle of your very good friends. They could mislead you and destroy your reputation. Be on your guard and watch carefully people that say the word 'my very good friend'. There is a term I use to denote friends that actually hinder your progress and mask it with sympathy and disguised love. I call them 'the drawbacks'. They gradually win your trust from years of input, only to destroy you when you need them most. They are the ones to mostly avoid because they could be your downfall. How can you allow them to interfere with your progress? It would be like laying a foundation of trust on unstable ground.

Parental influence can sometimes be a disaster in childhood dreams. If, for instance, my Dad wanted me to become a footballer, he should have given me the necessary advice on how to become the best footballer, but not force it on me. The best kind of advice you can give to a child is when you give them reasons for your choice and they accept those reasons. They should also be passionate about the whole idea in question. The worst kind of advice for a child would involve enforcing an unrealistic dream on him or her, only for them to realize a few years later it was all a mistake. It would be like the 'cries' of a motherless child, because to the victim it would be like embracing reality at the most unwanted hour. Parents should wise up when giving advice to your children, because that could be the beginning or the end of that journey in life. They see you as their masters, so therefore be very careful on how you advise and guide them.

Don't over spoon-feed them because that will only make matters worse, as I said earlier. Parents, listen to your children and embrace their dreams, but ensure you teach them. If parents share the same dream as their children, it normally becomes an explosive event. I have heard about many stars that became true stars due to a talent their Mum and Dad envisaged when they were young and acted on them quickly. As the child grows up, this talent then becomes second nature. The secret language of our minds ensures that those teachings keep us up to date and even bring out the best in us. Our learning abilities are amazing when explored, and that's how great men are produced. They ponder their imaginings and then make them happen, and that is how children can explore what's left out there. The 'chat-room boxes' are what I call the classic work colleagues who get themselves entangled with the gossips around the working environment. They always seem to have something to say and on every occasion seem to want to air their uninvited views. They tell all kinds of stories to the point where people either progress or regress. I am going to capitalize on the retrogressive aspect of our dreams. Most of us address work situations differently depending our circumstances. But remember, because of the little cliques at work it could be the start of a catastrophic journey. We all have dreams and strive to achieve them, but when we mix with people with different motives who have chosen the wrong path, it is left for you and me, who do know the consequences of 'wrong living', to correct them. I have found myself in certain situations at work, when, sincerely speaking, I should have left but, because of our modern wage system, it has become a fight for survival. Everything was done awkwardly and 'swear words' were dished out to everyone that was in the building. It was hard, but because man is a social being I had to find the best way to fit in. Cultivating certain habits that are very difficult to stop sometimes derails us from our dreams.

I have seen a lot of people fall apart due to work colleagues. They all team up as friends and explore different places and situations. Once you are out of the job, you are forgotten. How then do you keep abreast of such a situation once you have fallen victim to it? I believe that people should start believing in whatever they believe, keep pushing on, and stop creating opportunities for the 'opportunity perpetrators'. Work colleagues are essential in any part of our job cultures, but once you become a victim of a 'shattered dream', it then becomes another story in your life.

'Peer pressure' is another kind of factor that has eaten deep into the fabric of our society. With modernization and different cultural mixtures, it is bound to produce both positives and negatives. Peers do seem to dictate a child's behaviour and if this pressure centres on our ways of life, then it might be a struggle. The reasons lie in the evaluation of our origin: it seems that we have changed or evolved over the years. But are we evolving for the better or for the worse? I believe in certain ways for the better and others for the worse. I can point to many things, for example, the latest gadgets, that are pressurizing our peers. They have begun to fall into the sphere of identity crisis to the point where education to them is a 'nuisance'. At school, they play with their toys; at home they embrace every toy that comes to mind. How then do you educate a child honestly about life when he or she has consistently formed the habit of playing with his toys for years?

I remember one story about a boy who at the age of 28 still played his games from dusk to dawn. He basically ate, slept and lived with his game to the point were he even missed out on his dinner. If a child, as a result of peer pressure, pays such a heavy price as to miss out on the realities of life, I believe that is the beginning of a great challenge, especially to the parents, in terms of self-realization. Believe it or not, a child learns from his surroundings, and if he is constantly bombarded by different concepts without being instructed on how to deal with them, then he is bound to face many problems in life. I am not suggesting that kids should not play with their toys, but that you should be wise in how you set up the whole scenario when it comes to games. If a child's mind is bombarded with games for years, it will certainly become difficult to wean him off the self-acquired habits. Therefore ensure you know whom your sons and daughters are playing with, because such traits could emanate from there.

Another factor that has a positive effect on our dreams are the classroom habits. Classrooms are basically designed for learning and encouraging our young people to ensure that they achieve academically and morally. Most youths nowadays see the classroom as a playground and indulge in all sorts of youthful exuberances as they attend different lessons. The problem is that some of them have formed the habit of sleeping in the classroom because they feel that most of their lessons are boring. The ideology here is that since I am being forced to attend school, I will use the opportunity to go to sleep. But he does not know that as he sleeps, he misses out on important subjects, which probably could help him throughout life. Such students play on the minds of their teachers and parents, inventing different lies for every given situation. Many of them have formed groups and as a result have gone beyond the point of missing lessons to truanting from school.

My advice would be that, if Mr A and Mr B do not share the same dream, then Mr A should be cautious about how he associates with Mr B, because Mr B may not have the willpower to decide how to go about life. This forms the basics of selecting your peers at a very young age in life. Classroom habits are numerous, with some particular students sending the wrong messages to others, which might be misleading. Imagine a scenario where some students deceive others, only for those who have been deceived to find out that at the end of the term that they have failed their exams. It then becomes really astonishing how students can really behave sometimes.

If birds of the same feather flock together, then it is obvious why people suddenly change in character as a result of their newly found friends. Don't become the victim of classroom 'chatterboxes' that shoot off their mouths only to deceive you in the end. Become a being of self-admiration and excel amongst the many. Don't befriend those social values that are not friendly to our very existence, but rather approach them with caution. Be careful of inquisitive friends and keep them at 'arm's length'. Avoid the drawbacks of society and always reassure yourself that you are on the right track.

Do we share the same dream? When questions like these are asked, be sure you know what phase of life you are in. Don't get swept away by waves of disgust and shame. Instead, instil positive values in yourself and stand by them, and this will surely make you a better person. Being accountable for my actions has opened a lot of doors to an understanding of my life as it is. Please do the same.

Positive Lessons 19

- If we associate with the wrong crowd, then we are bound to stray from our path. Lesson: Be wise who you associate with.
- Friends could be your greatest assets towards self-discovery, but associate with the wrong ones and there is your downfall.
- We think about wealth as all there is in life, but believe me, achieving our dreams could be equated to our purpose in life.
- A person who disguises himself as a friend, only to set you back in life, must be branded as a 'drawback'.
- Laying a foundation of trust on shaky ground is a waste of energy and time.
- Please, parents do not enforce your dreams on your children, because it could be a constant reminder of their downfall.
- The mind understands what it has experienced: others, a strange phenomenon, etc.
- Great men ponder their imaginings and then make them happen.
- 'Chat- room boxes' are work colleagues that involve themselves with gossip that could ruin lives. Lesson: Avoid them at all cost. Beware of the opportunistic perpetrators and start living.
- How do you educate a child about life when he spends more than half of the day with his toys?

- The cost of all these habits could be the price that our society pays due to indiscriminate acts. This is a primary truth.
- Classroom habits have become a major problem in our educational system; our society is a perpetrator.
- If birds of the same feather flock together, then it is obvious why people suddenly change in character as a result of their newly found friends. This seems to be a common problem in our society.
- Don't embrace societal values that are not friendly to your very existence, but rather, approach them wisely,
- The revelation of the future can only come to those who wish for it.
- The choice of becoming a better person is left to us: be careful of a bad association or wrong approach.
- My belief in people stems from their actions 'their minds' is my prior concern.
- The reason for my distrust of people is their lack of understanding.
- Our dreams depict our state of mind; our actions test our character.
- If we understand the crux of our existence, our dreams could be history.
- Man's understanding of nature stems from his surroundings. His goal could come from his wishful thinking: a common approach.
- A shattered dream depicts the uncertainty of life, but on a closer examination it could be a door to an avalanche of opportunities.
- The truth about our dreams in life is that sometimes we are far from it.
- A step in the right direction is unaccountable, but those who achieve their dreams are the ones we talk about.
- The reason why we owe a lot to our dreams is the fact that they are an initiator of human struggle.

CHAPTER TWENTY

How do successful people stay on top?

We all have goals, but remember, when you get to the top, how do you stay there? You are in control of your success, so start now. When you think you are running out of steam, what is your next move? There are so many reasons why you can remain one of the most successful people on the planet. But work on those qualities that made you who you are. Do not neglect them, because your strength and weaknesses are still going to be tested along the way. Strengthen your weaknesses and make them your strengths.

Do not let your achievements mask your sense of judgement. At times man believes in himself but fails to realize that his pride could lead to his fall. Be wise and listen to people around you because, if there is a problem, they will be the first to know, but be careful whom you listen to because not all are happy with your achievements. I have searched for answers as to why people who are successful stay on top and the answer I always get is the drive towards being successful. There is the force that ensures that they stay focused and concentrate on the things that matter.

Successful men are normally wise and align themselves with the laws of the land.

They embrace the laws of the land and abide by them strictly. Not only do they have this drive but also the more they achieve the more the drive to succeed reveals herself. It is like an 'addiction' that drives men towards realization of their dreams; to me this is a 'positive addiction'. But be wise: do not be consumed by the 'drive to succeed' principles. My Mum used to say that to achieve is great, but when someone does not enjoy his trails of achievement, it becomes his downfall. My advice is that you enjoy every step of the way as you amass the fortune of success. If you lose your identity in the course of your success, then you have fallen to the 'ruins of wealth'. Man, as a being, has been given the gift of rationality; in effect, he is able to differentiate between right and wrong. If he chooses to fall to the ruins of his wealth then he can be classed as a 'foolish man'. Most of us strive to attain success in our everyday lives. But do we make an effort to ensure that we do not lose our identity? I have seen a lot of men fall to the 'ruins of success' as a result of lost identity. They become controlled by their success. Their arrogance is nothing to write home about. They step in everyone's way as they climb up the ladder of success and, to them; it is the order of the day. But my question is, when they attain to these heights, what makes them lose their self-identity?

The answer lies in the psyche of successful men who let their guards down and are controlled by the 'ruins of success'. A few successful men know what it takes to help each other; one of the reasons why we are all together on this planet is to help each other. It is of 'divine essence' that we help each other towards attending to our basic needs. This is one of the secrets of highly successful people; they brand it all in the name of charity. Don't you know that the law of nature promotes such acts of giving? My advice is, be wise about this, as wisdom consists in knowing where to stop so as not to overstretch 'yourself'. Be persistent, consistent and dedicated towards your life and you will excel in all endeavours.

The world we live in is dynamic so don't lag behind. In the past, it was all about the industrial age, but now it is all about computers. Are you at peace or at variance with the computerized world? Start now to familiarize yourself with it. A comment that passes my ears from particularly unambitious people is, 'I am not interested in this so-called computer age.' My question is, how does one intend to survive in the world governed by computers? It is very important for you to be on your guard about things around you. Maximizing the use of computers will help in achieving your dreams. If you are already on top, then you have to sharpen your motivation skills. Talk to yourself every day and seek advice when there is no way out. Always remember, someone helped you to get to the top. Don't suppress people around you because you feel you have achieved a lot. Always remember that your oppression of others can lead to your downfall. These are various reasons why some successful men may lose a lot of trust:

- Oppression of others
- Bad name
- Arrogance
- Living on the ruins of wealth

These among many other causes could lead to a man's downfall. Don't walk in the 'ruins of wealth', because it could be the start of another chapter in your life.

One of the reasons for success that I found is that most successful people understand how the course of nature works and how to deal with it. They invest highly in working out ways around their taxes, financial planning, and interaction with their business partners and how to invest in the current market. Financial management ensures that your money is under a tight network and that it is at all times performing at it very best in the money market. What do I mean? It means ensuring that at all times your investments are 'ticking over' and you are in control of what is happening. You entirely depend on the market structure and have learnt how the financial market works. Successful people never put their money in places they are not sure of. They ensure they have done most of their homework, by sorting out a lot of strategies of risks, and have consulted with the right bodies when it comes to investments and taxes. All in all, they set out on the journey that they know best. My question then is, what do you know best? But remember, it is not just about knowing that helps; you should be able to enforce your strategies, principles and efforts on people who are going to help you achieve your dream. One frequent pitfall of people who have tried and failed is that at times they do not know the science behind the whole business, but when it comes to enforcing these principles and strategies it becomes an even bigger hurdle. All I remember from my business lessons is that every individual in an organization must have a reason why they have been employed. It could be for motivational skills or management etc., but remember, you can't do everything. Some people have been trained to the highest level to ensure that work situations are in control and that projects meet their deadlines. Leave it for them to do, and don't become a jack-of-all-trades, because it wouldn't help sustain a business or lead to its growth. Successful men understand these facts, and that's why they keep striving for the best.

Another important fact is, before deciding on starting up a business, it is always wise to ask for legal advice to ensure you know what you are committing yourself to. It might all be too much because of the different laws and how they govern or control your actions. Always remember, they have been put into place for a reason. Don't fall into the trap of those who, because they didn't study the law properly, have fallen foul of the law. Start by first understanding the law around you, and then embrace every aspect of it. If you understand how the law works, you will definitely benefit from it as you engage in your business. Taxes date back hundreds of years to a time when they were paid in kind. Taxes kept kings or other rulers in control of the land, and with these taxes the land was constantly looked after by these monarchs. Nowadays, yes, the monarch is still in place, and these taxes are still used to ensure that the country is looked after. Make sure you study how the tax system works and how you can gain from it. There are books out there that can help you to become knowledgeable about such matters. Most successful men understand how taxes work and they work around them in order the get the maximum out of it. My policy is that if your want to engage yourself in any activity or project, do it very well. Don't become one of those who have fallen because they have tried so many things and in the end have given up. If you become one of those, you will never gain experience of anything and in effect you will become a failure even before you've started. Successful men plan, execute their plan and stay on course. They always know where they are heading, they 100 % believe in any project they have committed themselves to and once committed, they strive to achieve excellence.

Take a look at this example. Mr Paul decided to save £20 every day because he felt that he never knew when a rainy day might strike. So, he decided that he was going to embark on this saving strategy. A few months later, he decided he wanted to embark on a car-washing project, so he decided that the best approach would be to get a loan from the bank. He approached the bank and took out a loan of £5000. As far as he was concerned, he was about to achieve his dream of setting up a car wash. But Paul had not done his homework properly, because he never took his staff's bills into consideration for the first few months. The £5000 he had borrowed was only for his business; he had forgotten he had bills at home, and for the business to grow he would have to leave off working there for some time in order to establish his business properly. In as much as he had just started saving some money, which was still far from his supposed budget, he was able to find the extra cash he needed to see him through the first few months of re-organization. All in all, Paul, managed to keep the business afloat, but he had done it the wrong way and definitely the hard way.

First, he should have done a survey to find out how many cars there were in the area and how people felt about getting their cars washed. Roughly how many cars were there in the area of interest? The survey would have given him an idea whether it was going to be successful. He could have then calculated his finances from the beginning to the end. He should also have saved up for at least six months or a year so as to be able to manage his finances properly. Why do I have to say this? Millions of us go into businesses not realizing what it entails. We all flock towards millions of investments in order to better our lives, but unfortunately find ourselves struggling financially. If we had thought about it carefully we would have done it differently. There are so many businesses that have failed not because it wasn't the right business to do at that time, but because of an ineffective planning and management structure that had been put in place.

In the end, it all becomes another story of failure. We don't bear failure in mind when it comes to achieving; instead, we see it as the force that triggers off a more effective strategy when it comes to organizing a business.

Another reason why successful people stay on top stems from their objectives. Most investors or business owners have clearly defined goals that have been set out through different strategies and management plans. They know it's achievable and therefore go for it. The problem with most new investors is that they define their goals based on assumption and not facts. If you base any judgment on presumption rather than facts, it is obvious why you fail even before the start of the business venture. Ensure you do a survey, read books and seek advice before embarking on any project. Your goal in any business should be to build a solid structure that ensures that its organization exhibits excellence. If you check organizations with a reputation, they ensure that every facet of their structure, from reception to services, is a network, which is tightly controlled. Loopholes appear there when certain members of the team become uninterested or begin to slack in their duties at work. In such cases, the organization will fish out the culprits and then deal with them accordingly. My vision is clearly defined. What is your vision in life? The problems I have seen in my everyday life is that some people seem to want to invest, so they invest in everything that comes their way. This brings me back to addressing the issue of understanding the reasons for investing. In other words, they stupidly invest in several places, all in the attempt to making money from it.

My question is, how do you keep abreast of the drastic changes that take place at times in the financial world? The answer you will most often get is that their financial adviser would probably know when such a crisis arises. Remember, yes, your financial adviser is there to help you, but you are the one that has everything to lose if your millions go down the drain. Is it not your responsibility to know where your money is being invested? Don't adopt the attitude that someone will do it for you, because it doesn't work. So, be wise about that and stop shifting some of your responsibility onto others. Ensure you invest wisely and not investing without putting thought to it. Don't become a 'master of none' when it comes to investing. When investing, always think about risk management and ensure that you have safeguarded against that. Do not become one of those who foolishly invested everything they had, only to find out a few months later they had to start afresh. I will remind you strongly, that the psychological implications are many, so be wise and safeguard against such eventualities.

To invest involves a stepwise approach, so please don't disregard that long-term planning. It takes years to really come to terms with your plans, so please don't rush into anything just because you feel this is the time. Take every necessary measure to see that once you are out there, there is no turning back. I normally use this slogan 'to invest is to accept risk and all its ways'. Are you willing to accept the risks involved when it comes to investing? Take a moment to analyse the risks you would have to take and how you would manage the stress that comes with it. It's all about the mindset and this comes from training yourself mentally. Some people feel they can't cope with the stresses that come with investment and as a result of this shy away from investments. My answer for you today is that everyone of us on this planet can manage our stresses depending on how we look at life. Stress management involves a stepwise approach towards ensuring that in every situation you have an option. Most people will say, I deal with my stresses the best way I know. But there are books, videos, etc., that can help you when you feel that you are stressed. One method I have learnt over the years is to believe that it was a phase and that it would phase out with time. But ensure you make the necessary provisions to get out of it.

Don't get consumed by it, make sure you know the source and then work towards it gradually. I always remind myself of our boundaries of uncertainty, as I have said earlier. Life without uncertainty attached to it cannot be a life of multiple adventures. My advice would be to be careful when it comes to risk-taking.

Very often, you see people with passion for what they do. Most people would say that they got into a business because they like it and also because of the money, but they forget that after a while it could fizzle out. When you have passion for what you do it becomes part of your daily life. My passion for helping people and also working for the elderly especially, is what I find exciting when it comes to pharmacy. The thought that I am truly helping the community drives my passion. I believe in the course of true-life situations. What do you believe in? What I have found most intriguing is that, for every successful man, behind him there's a woman who nurtures him and fills his heart with love and through her, most of his works are expressed. If you think about most of the successful men on the planet, there is always a woman behind their success. It doesn't necessary means you can't become successful on your own. All I am saying is that a woman helps to ensure that all is going according to plan.

I believe that if you embrace success as your anthem, it then becomes your own. Nevertheless, 'nothing emerges from nothingness'; therefore, positive thoughts would definitely give you the armour to fight your battle. People think about chance, but it depends on what angles you are looking at it from. If you believe that one day your chance of becoming a millionaire will emerge without putting in an effort, then my advice would be 'think again'. There are millions of people out there, waiting for the exact same chance. If you try and work out the probability that it is going to fall on your doorstep, it would definitely be an uncertain event. On the other hand, if you take the chance when it comes to putting in a lot of effort towards a course of action, then I would say yes, at times if you are in the right place at the right time and fate is on you side, then probably your chance of becoming a successful person could be imminent. But leave all this and search for uninhabited niches out there that have not been seen. Successful people understand the difference between fate and chance, and that is something you have to understand when it comes to self-actualization.

Success is no secret, rather a platform on which those that desire to achieve exhaust all available options left to them. Success comes from the mind and hence expresses its 'aura' around those who 'actively' seek it out. I cannot overemphasize the importance of the hide and seek rule. As I have said earlier on, if you were to look at success from only one perspective then it wouldn't make sense.

Success encompasses all in life. You cannot separate health from life; therefore; to be successful ensures that you are in control of your life and circumstances.

Positive Lesson 20

- For every individual, there is this mark of achievement bestowed on him or her; it is only left for the individual to find it.
- Achievements are there for us to embrace. Do not idolize them; rather let them idolize you.
- Be careful about the people around you.
- This force, which ensures that successful people stay the course, is the force that I want you to reckon with. Think about this.
- The drive to succeed is like an addiction that drives men towards realization of their dreams. This is a positive addiction.
- Enjoy every step of the way as you amass your fortune of success.
- Man has been given the gift of rationalization and that is why he is able to choose between right and wrong.
- The arrogance of some successful men tells you a lot about them.
- Successful men who have let their guards down and are controlled by success are in the category of fallen men.
- It is of divine essence that we stay together and become our brother's keeper.
- Charity, charity, charity is one of the secrets of successful people. It is of divine essence to give to others who are less privileged.
- The world is changing and so are people. Be at your best at all times to ensure that you are aware of necessary changes.
- Laziness is not an excuse for your downfall; acceptance is the key to most of our problems. No matter where you go or what you see, do the right thing always and you will be surprised by your rewards.
- The laws of the land have been put in place for a reason; embrace them.

- If I were to define the 'ruins of success', I would say it is when you idolize wealth and get consumed by it.
- Those who climb the ladder of success through suppression of others could ultimately face their conscience at some point.
- People who invest without putting much reasoning to it, find that they only have themselves to blame.
- Planning is an essential part of success; time our intimate guide.
- Success comes from the mind and hence expresses its 'aura' around those who seek it.

CHAPTER TWENTY-ONE

A Concise Overview of the Introduction to Positive Life Lessons

Man has been born into this world in order to fulfil a purpose, and if this purpose in life is not fulfilled then we will have failed in the search towards revelation of mankind. If we bear in mind that life is the mystery behind all reasoning, it should be clear in our minds why our lives stem from a purpose. The problem with the common man is his lack of understanding of the reasoning behind man's existence. We seem to go for things that are out of reach rather than using the basic things around us to maximize our potentials. Man as he stands has 'hidden talents' and these are the qualities bestowed to him. For him to explore these, he first needs to understand the reason why we are here. The problem is that society as it stands has moulded us the way it wants us, but at times nature goes against those precepts. The question of complexes as it stands depicts the attainment of oneself. If we fully understand ourselves then we can rest assured that we would be able to face our challenges as they come.

Life is a state of struggle but it depends on the individual in question. He might perceive it as a state of struggle or as a place that has deterred man from his destiny.

There are so many questions that I normally ask myself and they come in the form of mysteries of life. One of the answers I usually find most useful is that man's understanding has been bridged to a certain degree, and beyond that degree reveals the boundaries of uncertainty. If man knew these uncertainties, life would definitely be a place of hell. In fact, the psychological implications would be disastrous. Nature has a way of cushioning these effects, if we circle around these boundaries; it is of prime importance that we do have a positive outlook for us to survive on this planet.

The course of our journey has been laid out, but I do believe that you can redesign the path you want to follow. The lessons of life are many, but those who fall under the ideologies of not living will find it difficult to self-actualize.

Since man has dominion over all things on this planet, it is left for us to carefully organize ourselves to reap the benefits of life. A dead man has no commitments and even amongst men has no will; this is the reasoning for living, and if we start living then life will be enjoyed to the fullest.

The problem most of us have is that we have neglected our health and consciously think everything is going to be alright. Remember, our body is made up of cells and for these cells to survive we have to look after every part of the body. If any part of it is in turmoil then we have to do our best to ensure that the whole being does not suffer. If not, there will come a time when the whole system might suddenly come to a halt. Please don't neglect the basic needs of man in pursuit of something artificial. Man has needs, and if these needs are not met then we are bound to pay a costly price and that is 'our life'.

Sacrifice is one of the virtues of life, which we all seem to have neglected. Sacrifices are made for a reason and that reason is piled up in stacks of rewards. If we want to get those rewards from our sacrifices then we have to do the obvious things first. Man has goals and these goals need to be ascertained, but if man does not understand the meaning of the word 'focus' then he is bound to stray from his path.

These goals are there for a purpose and therefore we should challenge our minds to ensure that we achieve our objectives. The problem with millions of souls out there is that their minds have been idle for years and, for them to effectively achieve anything, they need to first self-actualize.

The act of habit forming is easy, but when you want to give up that vice of yours it then becomes a problem. I always say this to my close friends: 'Don't start something you can't stop.' The reason is simple: we all know how strong we are when it comes to our willpower. Therefore, if you really care about yourself, try as much as possible to advise yourself at all times. On the other hand, to people whose bad habits have become a problem my advice is, start off on a daily basis to tackle your bad habits. The trick here is to know yourself and align yourself with your life.

There are so many reasons why successful people stay on top, but one of the reasons I find most useful is their drive towards achievement. It is like an addiction, which has maintained them on the path towards self-attainment. To me, it is like a positive addiction; to others it could just be a way of life.

The quest for our existence lasts from conception to death, and in between these phases lies the mysteries surrounding life. All those who reflect on their lives and act according to positive lessons of life will ultimately reap the benefits. Whether you believe this or not, to those who are about to self-actualize, my advice is to stay on course.

About the Author

Ifeanyi Onwuka is a Pharmacist in the UK. He graduated from the University of Portsmouth in England with Masters in pharmacy degree. He is happily married with one daughter. His childhood struggles and years of active learning phase in seminary school all reclaimed his mind towards modern psychology. With this, he developed the art of understanding the psychological needs of the modern society.

His career has diverted his focus on drawing out the positive elements in people and as a result of this decided to publish his first book, 'An introduction to Positive Life Lessons.'

Printed in the United Kingdom
by Lightning Source UK Ltd.
133300UK00003B/7-57/P

9 781434 366245